Wake Up to a Happier Life

FINDING JOY IN THE WORK YOU DO EVERY DAY

Wake Up to a Happier Life

FINDING JOY IN THE WORK YOU DO EVERY DAY

AMANDA DICKSON

SHADOW
MOUNTAIN

Salt Lake City, Utah

Visit us at ShadowMountain.com

Library of Congress Cataloging-in-Publication Data

Dickson, Amanda.
  Wake up to a happier life finding joy in the work you do every day / Amanda Dickson.
    p. cm.
  Includes bibliographical references and index.
  ISBN 978-1-59038-757-3 (hardback : alk. paper)
  1. Job satisfaction. 2. Satisfaction. 3. Conduct of life. 4. Self-help techniques. I. Title.
  HF5549.5.J63D53 2007
  650.1—dc22   2007008892

Printed in the United States of America
R. R. Donnelley and Sons, Crawfordsville, IN

10   9   8   7   6   5   4   3   2   1

To Aaron, the source of my joy

CONTENTS

ACKNOWLEDGMENTS

I am so grateful to everyone who ever hired me, who took a chance on an overly energetic woman when she promised she could learn to do the job. My bosses gave me so much more than a paycheck. They gave me rich experiences and, ultimately, the stories in this book.

In particular, I would like to thank Chris Redgrave, the general manager of KSL Newsradio. She has been my mentor, my teacher, my friend and sister through many years of growth and glory. I have learned more from watching her conduct a meeting than from most of my formal education. She helped me both feel and be competent.

I would also like to thank Rod Arquette, who hired me for the job I have loved the most and who has tolerated me through many changes in my life; Rodney G. Snow, who hired me for the job I loved the least and who taught me more than I thought I was capable of learning; Thomas Calloway, who hired me many moons ago and who trusted me with his restaurants; Starley Bush, who gave a law school dropout her first shot in radio; Roger Brown, who was the first one to tell me I could make a living using my voice; Dave Allred, who hired me to do the PA announcing for the Utah Starzz and then explained to me what that was; Greg Marsden, who trusted me with 10,000 screaming University of Utah gymnastics fans; Jay Shelledy, who let me, of all people, write a sports column for the *Salt Lake Tribune*; and Craig Wirth, who encouraged me and introduced me to teaching in the Department of Communications at the University of Utah.

I am also so humbled by the faith Sheri Dew has placed in me in agreeing to publish this book. I have admired Sheri and been inspired by her for many more years than I've known her in person and feel blessed every time I'm with her. I am deeply grateful to my longtime friend Jana Erickson, whose friendship I have enjoyed for nearly twenty years and who, lo and behold, agreed even after all that to be my project manager for this book. And I would like to thank Richard Peterson, my editor, for his wisdom and insight into this thrilling if not a little intimidating process of writing; designer Sheryl Smith for her work on the cover and interior of the book; and Laurie Cook for her typesetting skills.

Most of all, I would like to thank my husband, Aaron, to whom this book is dedicated. He makes my life and all of its wonder possible. He is the foundation and freedom of my life—he and my children. This book would never have been written if I hadn't been motivated by the news that I was pregnant to finally sit down and do it. My youngest son, Aiden, was born shortly after I finished the book. He, Ethan, Ashley, Cameron, and Laurel are in every chapter of this book and of my life.

INTRODUCTION

I love to work. I know that makes me a little sick and twisted, but I love it. I love the feeling of accomplishment, of being good at something, of connecting with my community. I love it for all the right reasons and some of the wrong ones. I love to provide for my family. I want to learn new things and try to think of ways to improve old skills. I love to make money and to help others make money. I delight in pleasing my boss, delivering for a client, or helping my children. I love to laugh while I'm working, whether I'm trying to resolve a dispute with a co-worker or picking up my son's stray socks in every room of the house. There is some funny stuff that goes on while we're working, which is definitely not limited to the hours of 9:00 to 5:00. (Dolly Parton should re-sing that song—nobody works from just 9:00 to 5:00 anymore, if they ever did.)

And if you're a parent—workin' 9:00 to 5:00 is a joke. Try 24/7! One of the hardest things for me to adjust to when I became a mother was that I could never take a break. There are no days off, no comp time, no off-sites with catered lunches, no sick leave—no recess. Maybe that's why the rewards are so sweet. Taking care of my children is the most thrilling and difficult job I've ever had and one I hope I can learn to do better.

I've had eighteen jobs in my forty-two years, and the main reason for all those changes is that I'm fickle. "Know thyself." Was that Shakespeare? Well I do . . . and I'm fickle. I'm the person who goes to Baskin Robbins and wants a taste of five flavors before I pick mint chocolate chip—again. When my husband and I have dinner out, I inevitably want his entrée more than my own and try to talk him into swapping. When someone asks me to do something, I say yes before I think of the ramifications. That way I get to do all kinds of things I have no business doing. And some of them I even get paid for.

I've been a waitress, a lawyer, a college professor, a disc jockey, a newspaper columnist, a restaurant manager, a WNBA arena announcer, a receptionist, a pizza maker, a sister, a daughter, a mother, a wife, and a radio morning show host. That is one of my current "jobs," but certainly not the only work I do. I'm on the radio every day from 5:00 to 9:00 A.M., and other than the initial shock when the alarm goes off at 2:45, I love my job. It reminds me of Meredith Vieira's first day on *The Today Show* when she said, "It feels like the first day of class and I'm sitting next to the cutest boy in school." I know just how she feels. I look forward to work every day.

And it's not just the work at the radio station that I love. I find joy in changing my toddler's diaper (what did I tell you about being sick and twisted?) just to see him all fresh and clean. I enjoy cooking for my teenagers—it's the only time they're actually in the same room together. I love helping my husband work out an idea he's been noodling, and I love supporting my neighbors and my community in whatever ways I can. These are all my "jobs," and I receive compensation in one form or another for each of them. Sometimes the compensation is in the indirect form of money and other times it's in the more direct form of joy. When I help my youngest son master a new skill (this week it was holding the spoon and scooping the applesauce himself), and I see the delight on his face, I am compensated.

It's hard to separate work from life. In fact, I'm not even sure why we try to do so. Maybe it's because we don't like our jobs or who we are when we're at our jobs, so we try to tuck that person out of sight before we get home to the people we love. We think, *Well, I need to be critical and demanding and insensitive at work, but I'd certainly never be that way with my children.* But the attempt to separate our worlds never quite works. We wind up complaining to our spouse about work, disconnecting from our children, dreading the next day. If only we could realize that work is a part of *all* life, not just the hours we put in at the office, and that when we improve the quality of our work, we improve the quality of our lives.

I used to think I enjoyed my job in radio so much because it's a great job. What's not to enjoy? Now, don't get me wrong. It *is* a great job, but I know of many other people who have what I consider to be great jobs who don't seem to love them. When I became a stepmom, I was nervous about taking on the role after all the nightmare stories I'd heard from acquaintances and had seen in movies about stepparents. I worried that no matter what I did, the kids would never respond to me, that I would always feel like an outsider, that the job would leave me wounded and insecure. Didn't happen. We've had challenges, of course, but the job of stepmother is a joyful and blessed job—one I wouldn't trade for anything and feel lucky to have. I get to love and care for three beautiful children, contribute to their lives, learn how to use my iPod in the comfort of my living room—and I never had to go through labor!

When I began to notice the disparity between the way I feel about work and the way my co-workers sometimes feel, the way I feel about parenting or dishwashing or mail-in rebate usage and the way my friends feel, I started wondering—*How is it that I have so much joy in my work?* Was I just born this way? Was it a full moon the night I was born or something? Is it that I eat too much sugar? Is the joy in the job or in me? Do I have similar joy when I'm peeling potatoes or stuck in traffic running errands or only at "work"? And what is "work" anyway?

If you're someone who dreads getting up in the morning to go to your job, resents the drive there, walks as slowly as possible to the entrance—I understand. If you struggle with taking care of your kids, feel overwhelmed and incompetent, wonder sometimes what you were thinking when you had children—I understand. I've had jobs I felt that way about. I still get that feeling once in a while now. But I believe there is a better way to work, to live. I believe there are tricks and truths that will help all of us have more joy in the many, many hours we spend laboring, whether in a workplace or in our homes.

The key is in the spirit we bring to the work. It's not about having the cool job, whatever that is. Your job is plenty cool, especially if you're a parent or someone who cares for children. Then your job is already as meaningful as it gets. The question is—who are you when you're doing it? Are you filled with resentment and bitterness, feeling trapped and wishing you didn't have to do the work you do? Or do you feel alive and grateful while you're doing it? This is the key, and I believe you control it. No new job, different kid, bigger house, or larger amount of money will change this one for you. In fact, nothing outside of you can do it. It's all up to you, which is the good news.

I hope you enjoy this book. Writing it was a labor of love for me, which is what I hope your work is for you. I hope you laugh while you're reading it. I hope you see yourself somewhere in it. I hope *work* is less of a dirty word and more of a pleasure when you're done.

Now—let's get to work!

CHAPTER ONE

"David, Why Weren't You David?"

"The more I want to get something done, the less I call it work."
—Richard Bach

etting: A spouse's work Christmas party or other social gathering anywhere.

"Hi. I'm Amanda."

"I'm Tom."

"Nice to meet you, Tom."

"This is my wife, Jill."

"Nice to meet you, Jill. This is my husband, Aaron."

"Nice to meet you, Aaron, Amanda."

"Jill. Tom."

Fidgeting all around.

"So . . . what do you do?"

Awkward pause. Apologetic expression. Followed by inadequate answer.

What do you do?

Why does that question freeze us? No matter what we do for a living, that question feels awkward, unwanted, anxiety producing.

When I was a waitress, I felt like my response should be, "I'm just a waitress." When I was a lawyer I felt like my response should be, "I'm a lawyer, but I'm a nice lawyer." When my sister stayed home to take care of her children when they were young, I remember how she struggled with answering the question with "I'm a homemaker." That didn't really say what she wanted to say.

Whatever our one-liner is, it doesn't do our work justice. Now that I'm a radio announcer, I don't know exactly how to say what I do. I'm not really a disc jockey. I'm not only a news anchor. Sometimes I say, "I wake people up in the morning."

"What are you—an alarm clock?"

"No, actually, I'm a radio announcer. I read news and talk about life on the radio every morning."

"Oh. That's nice. I don't listen."

I've thought about the question "What do you do?" so much. I've often wanted to answer it with something less expected, like, "I watch *Deal or No Deal* and eat takeout. What do you do?" Or "I read novels from the sale table and drink more Diet Pepsi than I should." Or "I spend most of my time obsessing about my children or my weight or both. How about you?"

Of course, "What do you do?" is often modified by "for a living?" "What do you do for a living?" is also an interesting question. I know that what the questioner is really asking is what do I do for money, but I take it more literally. What do I do to live, to sustain life and all that that means? That may include what I do for money, but it's so much more than that.

You may do a number of positive things "for a living." You may pray, love your family, take care of your parents, run in the early morning hours, look after your nieces and nephews, cook hopelessly fattening but delicious meals, commute two hours every day—one way. These are all things that you do to live, to enhance and sustain your life. You may also do a number of negative and destructive things to get through your life. You may abuse prescription medications, yell at your spouse, complain endlessly to anyone who will listen, blame your children for your mood, cheat your boss out of the time and talent he deserves from you, or cut people off in traffic. You may do these negative things just to get through the day. Somehow they feel as essential to your life as oxygen, even if you don't know why.

How often do you laugh? Do you smile easily? Do you smile at people you don't know or only people who sign your checks? Do you hang up the phone and ridicule your clients, or do you genuinely enjoy them for all their eccentricities? Do you go to parent-teacher night to get inside your child's world and learn about what she's learning, or do you do it because you're supposed to? It's not just about *what* you do for a living, it's also about *how* you do it. Do you do it with creativity and joy or do you do it with resentment and bitterness? What is the spirit of your work?

The place I want to start is talking about the kind of work you've chosen to do. And I want you to think about all of it, not just what you may do in an official workplace. Your workplace is wherever you are when you're working. Think of your life and all the labor that you perform. What jobs have you chosen? What projects do you take on? Right now, I am a mother, a wife, a neighbor, a radio announcer, a public speaker, a friend, and a writer. I am also a daughter, an aunt, a book reviewer, an e-mailer, and an occasional eBay shopper. I'm also a neglectful gardener, a pathetic housekeeper, and a self-deprecating cook.

This is the first step—looking at the work you do. It is definitely not the last step and probably not the most important step, but we have to start here because there may be a change a-comin'.

I remember hearing a story or reading it somewhere (sorry—I am a bookworm who has thousands of books, some of which are high enough up that my toddler has not yet managed to pull them off the shelves, and I can never remember where I read something) where a man reaches the end of his life and approaches the pearly gates, dazed and slightly apprehensive. When he gets there he is greeted by an angel with a calm and knowing expression.

"Hello, David," the angel smiles warmly.

"Hello," David manages to reply.

"David, I have only one question for you. Why weren't you David?"

The story has stuck with me. I have often asked myself, *Amanda—why aren't you being Amanda? Why aren't you living the life you were born to live? Why don't you sing more, paint more, listen to your teenagers more? Why don't you forgive easier, tell your husband how beautiful he is, be patient with your co-workers? Why don't you help people?* (I better quit before this turns into a Tim McGraw song. Not that there's anything wrong with that.)

Years ago, before I ever got into radio, people used to tell me, "Ya know, you have a deep voice. You ought to do something with that voice for a living." I was a law student at the time and hadn't the foggiest idea what they were talking about. I thought maybe they meant being a phone solicitor (a job I actually held for four hours—my shortest stint of them all), but that didn't wind up being something that suited me. In fact, the reason I quit the job after only half a shift is because I happened to call a woman who had just lost her husband the week before. I was cold-calling people, one after another from an assigned phone list, pitching vacation time-share condos in Hawaii—and I called a woman who had just lost the love of her life to cancer. She asked me through sadness but with strength, "Who do you think you are, calling a widow to sell some romantic vacation getaway in Waikiki?"

"I'm so sorry," I responded, unable to think of anything else to say.

"You ought to be," she replied, then hung up.

She was right. I was so sorry. And I quit on the spot.

When people commented on my voice after that, I figured out they were talking about doing radio or voice-over work for commercials. That felt a little strange, too. I didn't know whether to be complimented or insulted. "You think I should be a disc jockey? Uh, thanks, I guess." But when the umpteenth person mentioned it to me, I finally asked myself whether they were on to something.

I don't think there is any one surefire way to find your soul's work. I think there are a million ways, but this is one trick that might work. If there is a talent you have that people are always commenting on ("You're so good with design. You ought to design other people's homes." Or "You are so funny. You should be a comic." Or "You are the best baker. Move over, Betty Crocker. I'd rather buy your cakes any day."), then maybe you ought to listen.

And I do say "maybe" because it's entirely possible that you have real talent in an area that is not your soul's work. I think it's unlikely, but it's possible. What is more likely is that you have a gift in an area where your soul feels comfortable and right. You are a great mother because you were meant to mother and love children. You are a great teacher because that is what the Buddhists call your "right livelihood." You are a great daughter because you love caring for your mother, being with her, sitting by her side and hearing whatever she feels like sharing with you. You are great at cutting hair or writing letters or listening to a friend's problems because this is your soul speaking to you. "Hey! It's me! This is who I really am! This is David!"

The easiest way to have more joy in your work is to pick work that speaks to your soul. And this means work that speaks to *your* soul, not necessarily work that looks glamorous or that others would think is terrific or that makes a lot of money (although it may be all of those things). I like to begin with the questions—What wakes you up in the morning? When does time stand still for you or when do you lose track of time? What would you do even if you didn't get paid? What are you really good at? What would people pay you to do again? What gives you that feeling a football fan has when he hears, "Game's on!"? What is Christmas morning for you?

My thirteen-year-old son, Cameron, told me the other night that he had practiced his guitar for two hours. He had lost track of time, he said. Can you believe it? He used to dread every moment he sat at the piano, but with the guitar—he loses track of time. He's come such a long way since he got that guitar for Christmas. He's learned so much, and what's even more impressive is that he's *loved* learning it. I told him how proud I am of him and how happy I am for him. Who knows? Maybe there's an Eric Clapton or another "The Edge" (the lead guitarist for U2) in there somewhere. This may be Cameron's soul's work. If so, he'll need extra help from God. Think of the groupies!

What do you do in your downtime, after you're done with what you *have* to do? (I know you moms are laughing right now. "Done? Downtime? What are you, nuts?") But if you had to name something, what activity do you really enjoy? Forget the title. Forget for a moment the financial compensation. What do you love to do? When you have a bunch of things to do on your list, what do you do first? Which is the one you dread the least? Do you put off cooking and wind up getting takeout because you hate to cook? Or do you put off the shopping because you prefer to chop vegetables and taste for seasoning for twenty minutes? Do you help your kids with their art projects, carefully gluing on macaroni or super-gluing gummy bears together into a DNA chain because, secretly, you really enjoy this? What is it that brings you joy right now?

What came to your mind immediately when I asked that? Don't second guess and hyper-analyze it—what do you love to do? Whatever that is—how much time do you spend doing that every day? Okay, every week? And is there some way you can spend more time doing it, or doing some variation on its theme? Now—if money is something you want and need—the next question is, how do we figure out a way for you to do that thing you love and get paid for it?

I know many of you are thinking, *Sure. Sounds good. But I have to pay the bills, and I can't have some cushy job tasting chocolate covered cherries for a living in the foreseeable future.* I understand. And I say that we begin with what you do for a living because it is just the starting point. We'll consider in a minute how to have more joy in the most seemingly mundane and even disheartening job you can name. I think there is joy, and even humor, in the most difficult and devastating of jobs. In fact, there may be more humor there. Sometimes in the heaviest of jobs, where doing it gets so painful that the spirit craves light, humor comes pouring in if we let it— and that humor soothes the soul. I am reminded of the TV star Ray Romano commenting that he would have never made it as a comedian if his father had hugged him just once. It was the lack of affection received in his youth that brought out his humor. It was the

13

tough job he had as a son that made his job as an entertainer so much more natural and successful.

But for just another minute I want you to consider how you choose to spend your time because it is such an important choice. I remember my very best day at the law firm where I worked as a rookie lawyer for two years, eight months, and three days. My very best day during that time was the day I got my business cards and saw my name embossed in gold. It read, "Amanda Dickson. Attorney at Law." I've never read anything so fulfilling in all my life (until I saw my child's report card). I felt as though I had worked a lifetime to see those five words arranged just that way on that card. Looking back now, I wish I had just gone to Kinko's and printed up some fake business cards to give myself the thrill and skipped the rest of it. (Okay—that's not entirely true. As my friend Kurt says, "All roads lead to here." I'm grateful for the experience of practicing law, grateful on many levels.)

I share that story to argue the point that your title is unlikely to give you joy for more than a fleeting moment. If you want to be the boss, manager, mother, husband, CEO, CFO, executive director, editor, friend, director of sales—whatever—for the sole purpose of feeling the power in the title, think some more. Pray some more. Sit with it a little longer and listen to your heart. The title won't get you up in the morning. It won't keep you there late. It won't help you bring creativity and energy and drive to the job. The title won't make you feel love. Even the title of wife will wind up hurting you if your desire is just to be married to *someone* and you don't really love this man you're marrying. A title, any title, will only reward you, however shallowly, for a brief, shining moment. It will give you something cool to say when you're asked at a party, "What do you do?" And it's not worth the depleted life force that you'll pay for the prize.

The life force you'll pay is your joy. You give up joy when you spend your irreplaceable gift of time doing something that goes against your soul or fails to feed your soul. You find yourself trying to compartmentalize. "Well, I have to do this for work, but then I get the weekend where I can really 'be myself' and love my life." Look at how many of your friends or co-workers live for the weekends. They even say, "I'm just hanging on until Friday. I can't wait for the weekend. TGIF!"

When you do work you don't love because you thought you should be a director, stockbroker, dancer, bus driver, or _____ (fill in the blank with whatever job you thought you wanted but really didn't), you eventually begin to rationalize: "Not everyone can have a job they love. Maybe I just didn't luck out in this life." "I make a lot of money, though, and at least I get to drive a Beemer and shop at Nordstrom. That's worth something, isn't it?" "There are a hundred people lined up to take my job. If I leave it, how will I replace it?" These are the excuses you make, and your soul dies a little with every telling.

David, why weren't you David?

I do believe that we allow ourselves to live so little in this life, maybe out of humility, maybe out of insecurity, maybe out of a lack of the ability to dream big. One of the things I've learned from interviewing famous people over the years is that there is mainly one difference between us and them—they went for it. From Marvin Hamlisch to Mike Wallace to William Shatner, they all impressed me as regular, interesting, and interested people who, rather than sit and wonder how other people did things, just did them. They risked it. They showed up when others were too sluggish or scared.

Are you doing what you were born to do? If so—God bless you. Pass it on. If not, if there is a longing in your heart to do something else, be involved in some other activity or endeavor, then what are you waiting for? If you yearn to be a better wife, to show love to your spouse in a way you don't currently do, what are you waiting for? Don't tell me you're waiting until the kids are grown up. J. K. Rowling wrote *Harry Potter and the Sorcerer's Stone* in brief snatches of time with her toddler sleeping in her stroller nearby. Don't tell me you're waiting until you lose weight. Oprah. Don't tell me you don't have time. The former governor of Utah and the state's first female chief executive, Olene Walker, got her Ph.D. by studying in the middle of the night while raising a boatload of children and loving a supportive husband. There is time for what we can't live without.

What can't you live without? What is your soul's work? What do you long to be doing for a living?

CHAPTER TWO

There Is No "Just"

"Nothing is really work unless you would rather be doing something else."

—JAMES M. BARRIE

I don't care *what* you do for a living. You can choose to run for the legislature, be a chef, work for Google, take care of your family, write for the newspaper, pick up the garbage and recycling, draw blood, arrange flowers, check out groceries—it doesn't matter. The "what" is not important. The fact that you are doing your soul's work, or work you can put your soul into, is. I've heard so many people describe what they do for a living almost with an apology. I've heard myself say these words too. "I'm just a radio announcer." "I'm just a mom." "I'm only the stepmom." "I'm just a secretary or a car salesman or a night manager." When I heard myself expressing such feelings, I used to think, *Well, that's just humility, Amanda. That's a good thing.*

I don't think so anymore. That's not the soul's truth. The soul wants to work, to be proud of the work we do, to think of the work we do with joy and energy. I am not *just* a radio announcer. I am blessed with the most wonderful job where I get to wake people up and be a part of their lives every day. I get to share information with them that they need—about their commute, about the weather, about breaking news, about insights into their world. I get to share stories with them about my kids and my life. I get to be a part of their lives and often receive a humbling amount of affection from them in return. I'm not just a radio announcer—I'm a friend to thousands of people, all by virtue of this job. How lucky is that?

And I'm not *just* the stepmom. Being my three older children's stepmother is a role I cherish. I have complete respect for the fact that I am not their mother, that I could not and would never try to replace their mother—but that doesn't mean my role isn't an honor and isn't significant. I get to love these children. I get to be in their lives, listening to them talk about school, helping them dream big dreams for the future, feeding them breakfast on Saturday mornings and dinner on Tuesday nights, keeping the pantry stocked with muffins and bananas for them. I've learned more from my stepkids about myself, about what matters to me in my life, than I have from any other teacher. I am so grateful to them, and to their father, for letting me be in their lives.

There is no "just." All work feeds the spirit, or all work *can* feed the spirit. Even washing the dishes can feed the spirit. I like seeing the kitchen and dining room slowly emerge from the aftermath of a meal. I like being able to ignore my kids for a few minutes while I'm rinsing off plates and scouring pots. (Okay—I'm only partially kidding there.) I like the challenge of fitting everything into a dishwasher too small for a single person, let alone a family of six. I like wiping the counters off when it's done, scratching the burned cheese off the stove, refilling the dog's bowls, and then turning off the light. Ahhhh. Mission accomplished.

I have felt that way about doing laundry, weeding, bathing the baby. There are some nights when I'm so tired I can't bear to bathe the baby, and I think to myself: *Well, how many baths a week does he really need? He wasn't playing in mud today or anything, and* most *of the strained peaches are out of his hair. It's not like he has a job interview tomorrow. One more night without a bath won't kill him.*

And then I remember the look on his face when he splashes me, the way he smells when he's really clean, and how much better I sleep when my body is warm and clean—and I start running the water.

There is definitely joy in that work.

There is joy in every form of work, I believe. I am sure the governor feels joy when he signs a bill he's fought hard for or finishes a long day of important meetings or represents the state well with dignitaries from around the world. I'm sure a lobbyist feels a sense of accomplishment when he skillfully uses the sixty seconds he's allotted to persuasively articulate his client's position. I know when I was a lawyer, the vast majority of what I did every day was not what I would call joy-inducing. I spent my time mainly arguing, in person and on the phone. I looked for what was wrong with other people or for weaknesses in a given position, and then I tried to exploit what was wrong. These were not endeavors that fed my soul.

But even in that environment, I do remember moments of joy. I would sometimes work on an argument for weeks—reading dozens of cases, writing and rewriting paragraphs, trying to anticipate every possible opposing point of view, taking the judge's prior decisions into account. I remember one case in particular that I worked on with a number of other lawyers in our firm. It was a complicated and important case that would affect the lives of the members of a young family. We represented the plaintiffs, and the insurance company's lawyers on the other side filed somewhere around twenty motions—motions to dismiss, motions to suppress, motions, motions, motions. As the rookie in our office, I did most of the initial grunt work in drafting our responses. I still remember the feeling I experienced when I finished the sixteenth memo in opposition to the motion to blah, blah, blah. It was euphoria, or as close to euphoria as my spirit could get in that line of work.

Sometimes it is the simplest work that gives us the easiest access to the most tangible joy. I think the big, beautiful jobs can be like Christmas. There is too much build-up and expectation, and the end result is never as good as the dream. But a good shave? Now you're talkin'. No matter whether you're a man or a woman, you feel a little sense of satisfaction after a particularly good shave. Ahhhh. No bumps. No little red marks. No nicks. Just close. Really close. And smooth.

You can get that feeling from getting the garbage out before the garbage man comes. Just once you want not to be caught in your pajamas as you hear the truck starting to head down your street. And on that one time when you remember to put it out the night before, and it doesn't storm and blow anything over or strew your trash on your neighbor's lawn, you feel such a sense of accomplishment. Ahhhh. The house is free of trash. The little garbage cans have been emptied from every room into the big garbage can, which was then tied neatly off and put into the enormous garbage can in the garage. The recycling has been divided out and put into the blue can. And the yard refuse, weeds, and grass clippings are in the bright green can. All garbage present and accounted for. How fulfilling.

Does it get any better than that?

I'm not sure I've ever thought of talking about shaving or taking out the garbage when someone asks me, "What do you do?" But they are forms of work, aren't they? Isn't everything we do, other than sleeping, work of some kind? If we're showering, we're working. If we're reading, we're learning. It might also be relaxing work, but it's work—it's doing something with the precious time we've been given. For many men I know, working in the garage or the yard is more relaxing for them than sitting still. For many women I know, the same is true, only the work is doing laundry, crocheting, caring for a parent, or gardening. And here's the thing—once you get it in your psyche that there is joy in the shaving, the jogging, the cooking, the writing of memos, and the attending of client conferences—you get it. It applies to everything, and you're on your way to a whole new quality of life.

I remember when I was working as a waitress. I would sometimes hear people refer to my job as being in the "service industry." I listen to *The Wall Street Journal* economic report every morning now as I drive into work at 3:30 A.M. (unless it's December, and then I listen to Christmas music). I often hear the reporters refer to the "service sector" or "service sector jobs" being affected, or not affected, by recent economic changes. I think I know what they're referring to—waitresses, hotel bellhops and clerks, maids. But aren't we *all* in the service industry? What industry does not serve someone or all people if you look at the bigger picture? Aren't teachers in the service industry? Aren't TV reporters and police officers and military personnel? Do we not refer to politicians as public servants (at least when we like them)?

Every parent is obviously in the service industry. Everything we do is about our children. When we go to the grocery store or gather up the laundry or clean the house, we're serving them. When we live good lives, when we go to work on time every day, we're serving our children. We are serving them when we feed them breakfast, even when we're exhausted; when we give them the only five-dollar bill we have in our wallet; when we buy what they need before we even think about ourselves. Breathing is serving them.

Does thinking of your job as being in the service industry change the way you think about it? Does it make you like it more or less? I saw Jon Bon Jovi on with Oprah the other day, and he was talking about going to Louisiana and seeing the people who were moving into homes being built with his million-dollar donation to the victims of Hurricane Katrina. He got emotional when he described how it felt to be hugged by a twelve-year-old boy who could barely get out the words, "Thank you for my home." He thanked Oprah for giving him the opportunity to touch the people affected by his money. And I thought, *Yeah. Wouldn't that be the best part of having lots of money—being able to help people? And wouldn't that feeling be incredible?*

Some of you probably know that feeling on a big scale. But all of you know it on some scale. If you've ever donated even one cent to United Way or any other charitable organization, you've served people. You served the woman you let cut in front of you in traffic, and you served the person you smiled at walking down the street. You served the mother and the toddler you waved in front of you in the grocery store line, and you served the guy at the gym you offered your stationary bike to when you were finished. We are all in the service industry. And maybe knowing that will give us just a smidgen of what Jon Bon Jovi felt on that sunny fall day outside of New Orleans.

I've been in management twice in my twenty-plus years in the work force. Once when I was in my early twenties, I was the night manager of a Western Sizzlin' Steak House. I was so honored to be given the responsibility, and I worked my behind off. I filled in for teenage cooks who didn't show up, bussed tables, refilled the salad bar, and learned how to cut meat. (Now there's a skill I'm proud of. There is something really fulfilling about knowing your T-bone from your rib eye.)

More recently, I was the program director for a radio station, one that I loved and helped create from scratch. It was a talk radio station for women, and it was wonderful. It was wonderful because of the amazingly talented people who turned their lives upside down to come to work with me. It was wonderful because of its pioneering nature and spirit. But the station didn't make it. Its failure surely wasn't due to a lack of effort or lack of love of the work. It just didn't get the ratings necessary for a radio station to survive.

The reason I bring this management experience up is because I remember when I was in the position to interview people for jobs. Nearly everyone I met with would tell me he or she was a "people person."

Interviewer: "So, what are some of the strengths you would bring to the job?"

Interviewee: "Oh, well, I'm really a people person."

Interviewer: "Okay. What does that mean in your opinion?"

Interviewee: "You know. I'm really good with people."

Perhaps it was because I interviewed so many applicants and hired an entire staff of twenty in just two months' time that I became overly sensitive to meaningless phrases, but "people person"? What is that? I know it means you think you're good with people, but could you be a little more specific? Are you good with people because you care about them, joke with them, compliment them, find ways to help them, ask them about their kids, tell them they have spinach in their teeth? What?

Think of what the opposite would be. You're a "thing person"?

Maybe there are some code-writing guys who truly work only in the middle of the night and prefer text messaging and e-mailing to any phone or, heaven forbid, face-to-face communication. I'm sure there are. You may describe yourself that way. But on 9/11, we were all "people persons." Maybe some of us are people persons at a technological distance when possible, but we're still people persons.

I do, in fact, think of myself as a people person—I just know I'm not unique in that regard. I love my interaction with my co-workers. Not as much as some, but more than others. I'm one of those who likes to get home to family as soon as I can, so shooting the breeze about the latest Sean Hannity rant is not as important to me as getting to the parking garage and on my way. I've been known to excuse myself right in the middle of someone's thought and exit stage left. Is that rude? I don't think so. If the person were telling me about a personal problem and needed my time and help, I would stop and give them my full attention. It's just that when I'm given a choice between shooting the breeze and being with my kids, the breeze is gonna blow right on by every time.

That doesn't mean I'm not a people person. I'm just not an hour-long fantasy football conversation kind of people person. I care about my co-workers' children. I want the people I work with to feel good about themselves and be successful in their jobs. I want to help them laugh when I can—if they want to. I like caring about them. It enriches my experience at work and makes me better at what I do. I like caring about my clients, too. When I care about them, their businesses, the families those businesses support—I do a better job for them.

It's like the Native American philosophy about the circle. I think of it as a version of "what goes around, comes around." I've heard the philosophy described as "What you give to the world on one side of the circle winds up coming back around to you on the other side." If you give out love and encouragement to the universe, they will find their way back to you, sometimes in unexpected ways. I think of this philosophy as the theme of the movie *Pay It Forward*—where the young student decides to change the world by doing something good for three people, and then encourages each of them to do likewise, and so on and so on.

No matter what we do for a living, we're not in it just for the money. There are people involved, starting with ourselves. I think some of the most unhappy workers I've ever known have been people who felt trapped, who felt that they had no choice but to keep jobs they hated, working for people they didn't respect, because they needed the money. They had children to feed. They had mortgages to pay. They had no other skills. This is what they thought. But I don't think that belief is true on a couple of different levels.

First of all, there are as many different ways to earn money as there are individuals to think them up. Whatever you're doing right now, it's not the only thing you could do to earn money. You could invent the next Post-it Note, or bake the next Mrs. Fields cookie, or move and get a job in an entirely different state. You're not trapped. You may be lacking somewhat in imagination, but you're not trapped. If there's a way to get out of the net, you're not trapped, and there are more ways to escape than you've ever dreamed of.

I know some of you have been telling yourself this story of being trapped for so long that it feels like it must be true, but it's not. It's familiar, it may be ingrained, but it's not true. Now—I'm not saying you should up and quit tomorrow. What I'm saying is you can. You can find a way to learn another skill in your off hours. You can find people who need help, and help them (and probably yourself in the process). And before you even start thinking about how to change your circumstance, the most important thing you can do is change your heart. If you want to stop feeling trapped, then stop it. Just stop it. It's like the guy who is hitting himself in the head repeatedly who says, "I wish I could stop hitting myself in the head." Then do. Stop it.

Begin to see the blessings in your current circumstance. That decision in and of itself may change you so profoundly that you may not want to change your outer circumstance. And that decision is always more important than changing your outer circumstance, which, no matter how many times you change it, can still feel like being trapped if your inner voice hasn't changed. You'll just feel trapped in a different cage if you don't change your outlook on this issue.

Haven't you known people at work who just aren't happy no matter what? The boss she can't stand gets fired, so she resents a co-worker instead. The co-worker quits and moves away, then it's the personnel director who makes her crazy. The disgruntled worker gets promoted, and it's the kids she has that force her to work in the first place. These unhappy individuals think they're slaving away for the money, but they're not. They're working for the payoff they get from being miserable every day. I don't know what that payoff is, but it's big. Bigger than their paychecks.

Maybe they like the safety of waiting for circumstances to somehow miraculously change. This is an easier stance to take than to really go after their dream. "If I hadn't had my kids so young, I could have finished college and gotten a better job." "If my wife made a little money, I wouldn't have to work so much overtime and never get to be home." "If my family didn't need so much money,

I'd be able to stand up to my boss without the fear of being fired." Does any of that sound familiar?

But none of those rationales is the real reason you're in the job you're in, is it? You're doing the job you're doing, with the attitude you're doing it with, because it's your choice. That's just the truth. If you're not enjoying your job, that's a choice, too. You could change your spirit tomorrow if you wanted to. Yes, you need to earn money, and I believe you when you say you can't think of anything else you could do. What I say in response is—keep thinking. Keep praying. In the meantime, go to work every day with the most positive attitude you can muster, and keep asking yourself, *What if this happened? What could I do with this idea? What have I learned today? Wonder how he does it?*

Let "just" and "have to" fall out of your vocabulary. You aren't "just" a clerk and you don't "have to" go to work. You are blessed with a job where you get to serve people, including yourself, your family, and your boss, not to mention your customers, every day. And you don't have to go to work—you *get* to, you *choose* to, you *want* to. How do I know you want to? Because you go! If you didn't want to go to work, you wouldn't. That would be my big clue that you don't want to go. As long as you're still going, it must be because you want to. You'd rather go to work than not eat or look for another job or ask your mother for money. Bravo! I like that attitude.

See—this stuff isn't so hard. Just because you've never done it before doesn't make it hard. It makes it unusual maybe, but not hard. Eating sushi isn't hard. You dip it in the wasabi and the soy sauce and pop it in your mouth. You don't have to use the chopsticks. A fork is fine. Now—the experience may be unusual. You may not have done it before, but it's easy. So is thinking about your work differently. It's easy, it's just unfamiliar.

I've heard people talk about how change happens in an instant. It doesn't take years and years of effort, even months of grueling pain and suffering—it happens in the instant the mind is truly made up. Yes, it happens again the next day and the next as you make decisions that affect your life—but the real change just happens. Think about it. The day you decided to propose marriage, you were ready. You knew you were going to do it—somehow. You might have been scared out of your wits, but you knew what you wanted. The day you decided to quit your job, same thing. The day you decided to go after the promotion, same. The day you decided to love your stepchildren, same. You live that change every day with the decisions you make, but the change happened in an instant—a precious, glorious, divine instant.

So—pass the wasabi.

CHAPTER THREE

The Spirit You Bring

"Pleasure in the job puts perfection in the work."
—ARISTOTLE

Perhaps the most important job in any company is the position of receptionist. She (and in my experience it usually is a "she") makes the first impression and likely a lasting one on you. If she answers the phone with warmth and interest, you feel heard. If she greets you when you enter and directs you with ease and grace, your experience with the company is positive before you even take care of business. I don't know how much money the receptionists at my company make, but it's not enough. Their contribution to our reputation and our clients' experience with us is huge.

I work at a broadcasting company where four radio stations and one television station are headquartered. People call our receptionists for the most amazing things. I sometimes think they get us confused with 411, or maybe 911.

"Hello, KSL."

"Ah, yes. We're planning a wedding a week from Saturday and

just wanted to know if it's going to rain so we can make arrangements for an indoor reception if necessary."

"Hello, KSL."

"Yes. I couldn't get in to the station this morning, but Amanda Dickson said something that was totally wrong. She doesn't understand the first thing about identity fraud or what the HIPA laws require. Our state government has totally dropped the ball here . . ."

Meanwhile, the phone keeps ringing and the receptionist tries to field each call with graciousness.

"Would you like Amanda's voice mail so you can leave her a message?"

"And another thing I wanted to say about Hillary Clinton. That woman has no business running for anything but the border . . ."

"Hello, KSL."

"Would you tell the President to shut up and stop interrupting *As the World Turns?* If I wanted to watch the news, I'd turn on cable. I WANT MY SHOW!"

"Thank you so much for calling. I'll make sure he knows."

"Hello, KSL."

"Yes. I don't mean to be rude or anything, but you've got to tell that anchor on Channel 5 to do something about her hair. I mean, does anyone look in the mirror around there before they go on television? It's awful!"

"Thank you so much for calling. I'll make sure she knows."

I do judge a company by their receptionists, and I'm really proud of ours. We have seven or eight of them, and they're all wonderful. They are patient and articulate and helpful. They even look great. You know the kind of women whose earrings match their belts match their shoes? That's them. They remember people's names, have the sense not to let loonies back in to see me (or anyone else), remind me tenderly when I'm late, forgive me when I drop the ball. They keep people in the waiting room from feeling uncomfortable when we're running behind, soothe the savage beast, encourage the young applicant who's there for a job interview. I see them with a phone in each hand, in addition to the headset they're wearing, and a smile on their faces every day.

I don't love them as well as I should, but I have an annoying and hopefully endearing habit of singing the name of one of our receptionists when I see her. Her name is Naoma, and whenever I see her, I go into full operatic obnoxious "Naooooommmmaaaaaaa!!!!" with arms flailing and hands hamming it up for applause. When I do this, she grimaces and gestures for me to cut it out, which only leads to a bigger crescendo. I do this *La Traviata* moment even if there are people standing in front of her desk. I do it *especially* if there are people standing in front of her desk because I want her to know "I see you."

I'm amazed at the people who have worked here for ten years who don't know the name of our receptionists. If I were one of the receptionists, I don't think I could stand it.

"Uh, you may have noticed me as you fly past my desk on your way to coffee ten times a day. I have a name. It's not Lovely or Hey There or Girl! It's Naoma!"

But of course, she's far too gracious a person to ever point out the obvious like that.

I bring this up because we've all had the experience of being treated with dignity and professionalism by a receptionist, and it's likely most of us have had the opposite experience as well. You've stood in front of a receptionist who is going on like this . . .

"Yeah. I know. Then did you hear what Alexis said? [Laugh] I know."

She has eye contact with you for a fleeting second as if you're blocking her direct sunlight, and then, after your presence has had no impact whatsoever . . .

"So, what did her boyfriend say then?"

Maddening, isn't it? Don't you just want to do something like clear your throat loudly or start talking as if she's listening, or better yet, loudly slam a stack of magazines down on the coffee table, maybe just walk right on back into the office until you find someone who cares that you're present? These situations are particularly excruciating when you're there to give them money. You're there to pay them, hire them, in some way give them business—and they still don't care. Where are we? Russia?

So the point is this. Same position. Same importance to the customer. Totally different spirit on the part of the employee. What can we attribute that to? Does the attentive receptionist make more money? It's possible, but I doubt it. Does she have a nicer husband at home? I hope so, but that wouldn't account for it. Does her employer set a higher standard for this important position? Likely, but that doesn't explain it either.

The difference is in her, in the spirit she brings. One of the receptionists at my work is named Gay. She has the most attentive and delightful personality you can imagine, even in the midst of insanity—perhaps especially in the midst of insanity. On heavy news days, the phones go crazy at a news station, as you might imagine. Makes sense. Most of the hundreds of calls are from people who are concerned, not sure they heard what they thought they just heard, and they can't wait for us to announce it again—so they call. She will patiently repeat fifty times in a row, "Yes. A bomb went off. We don't know about injuries yet. We'll announce it as soon as we know." She says this each time with sincerity and without any irritation. I've often thought that she treats every caller the way she would want her mother to be treated—with the same care and respect. What a blessing she is to this company and to me personally. She notices when I'm not feeling well even before I've told anyone. She's just attentive that way to the spirits of those around her. This is who she is. She brings that level of engagement and that desire to contribute with her every day. And while I'm sure she doesn't work as a public service, her work goes so far beyond what is required in her job description.

All work can be done with creativity and joy. I've seen a single mother of three, who is dancing as fast as she can, take time to make dinner for a sick, pregnant co-worker. And not just any old dinner, although anything would have been appreciated, but a turkey and mashed potatoes dinner with the works. I've seen custodians in my children's schools lovingly polish the floors, ushers at the university stadium take tickets and greet fans with genuine warmth, and cashiers at the gas station say good-morning with a lilt that implies they really are grateful to see you. I've seen parents throw birthday parties for their children with attention to every detail, every balloon, invitation, and lawn sign that announces in bright colors "Party Here!"

And with each of these individuals I've realized it's not the job that's making them happy. And it's not that each of them has it easy in life either. They're not rolling in dough. They probably have issues with their kids and co-workers like the rest of us. Their car might not have passed inspection this month or maybe they blew out a tire on the way to work. Their mother's health may be failing, and they feel helpless sometimes. And yet they are joyful, so joyful that they have enough to share with the people they encounter while they're at work. They are a gift to their families and to the rest of us.

If it looks as though their positive attitude comes easily to them, that's only because they've probably been wise for a while now. They likely figured out some time ago that you can live this life like a pig going to the slaughter, or you can hold your head up and give as much joy as you can muster. They've learned that eight hours is eight hours, whether they make every second miserable or find a way to take pleasure in their work. And they've realized that when they are affable and courteous at work, that attitude carries through to their home life and they're naturally better parents and spouses.

They just get it.

Even if you're not one of these people, you've seen them. Maybe you're lucky enough to work with one. And maybe you work with one who is the opposite—the kind of person who you'll go around the building to use a bathroom in the other wing just so you don't have to walk past that person's cubicle—because one conversation with them and you're done. You're exhausted. You have no energy left for your job or your kids or even stopping at the store on the way home. This person is just one of those lost souls who sucks all the oxygen out of every room she's in. God love her. She's been complaining about her ex for so many years you can't even remember when she was married. Or he's been resenting his supervisor for so long, the supervisor has been promoted, two times, and has since retired.

They're stuck, these poor lost souls, and I've been one of them myself. I remember shortly before I quit a job I had years ago, I couldn't feel anything positive about the place. My boss didn't appreciate me. My co-workers were self-absorbed whiners. (Talk about the pot calling the kettle black.) I didn't make enough money. The hours were too long and always on holidays. Blah. Blah. Blah. I must have made everybody miserable for miles around, especially my good friends, who listened to me go on and on for as long as they could before their schedules all started to get too full to see me.

I'm not proud of my attitude then. It's almost hard to believe she was the same woman I am now, but the memory is clear. And it had nothing to do with the requirements of my job. My job was actually great. Hundreds of people would have taken my job in a heartbeat, moved across the country to take my job, been thrilled for the opportunity. The problem was in my spirit, not my circumstances.

Every time I hear people complain about their jobs I think of this, and I remember that I've heard people even in the most glamorous of jobs complain. Movie stars lament being famous for all the trouble and restriction of movement it brings. Sports figures resent the boos directed at them by their opponents' fans. Media people resent the criticism of their abuse of their own power, even as they choose without justification to cover one story instead of another. Even mothers and fathers, blessed with the greatest job of all, complain about having to take care of their children.

This last one breaks my heart, and I've heard it enough to not be shocked by it anymore (which is itself shocking). I've heard parents complain about everything from making dinner to washing clothes to paying for school fees. I've heard parents whine about never getting to go out, having to pay babysitters, or needing to postpone vacation plans because of a sick child. And I think of girlfriends I've had who so desperately want to have children and for whatever reason cannot, and I weep.

Think of the difference in the quality of the food, in its actual nutritional value, and the way it's digested in the following two scenarios. The first meal is prepared by a mother who makes dinner while muttering complaints about her husband and her children, slamming plates down on the table, picking at her own food while making certain everyone knows she's mad. ("If they're not here and sitting at the table when this dinner is ready, it's all going straight in the garbage!")

Contrast that with the mother who sings while she works, stopping to pat her youngest on the head and shoo her away from the stove, says a blessing over the food before her family eats and thanks God for her husband and all he does for his family. ("I'm so grateful we can afford to buy this good, healthy food so I can help my children live strong and well.") I just know the children of those two families receive different nourishment even if the calories are identical.

Teenagers are notorious for a whining, roll-the-eyes attitude, and sometimes mine are no exception. I think there is something that fires off in the DNA when a child turns thirteen, something that lies dormant those first twelve years, waiting to come out and strike, something that must be essential to the maturing process. Suddenly everything is boring, everyone is irritating and stupid, every job is a chore that can't be tolerated. And it makes the importance of the difference in attitude so clear. Especially when they've just turned thirteen, and the helpful days of eleven and twelve are not so long ago that you've forgotten. You remember when they would help you in the yard just because you were out there and they wanted to be with you. You remember when they would make their bed because you asked them to, tell you about their day at school, watch a movie with you without saying, "This is so stuuupiddd."

Then something happens internally, and they expect to be paid for getting out of bed.

"Hey, son, can you help me mow the yard Saturday?"

"Sure. Will you pay me?"

"I pay you an allowance."

"That's not for mowing the yard."

"What's that for?"

"For the privilege of being my father."

"Oh."

I don't know who I feel sorrier for in this scenario, the teenager or the parent. To need and want your child's help and not get it is tough, frustrating, even sad. You start to feel jealous of your neighbor, whose teenager is outside mowing the lawn. You can hear the mower through the open window. But to not feel like helping your father must be worse. I see the discomfort in my teenagers sometimes when their dad asks them for help and they refuse or go about the task with a sullen look on their face. They're not quite mature enough to know that if they could be generous in their spirits, they would feel so much better.

I have faith that they'll learn this lesson. I already see sparks of clarity from time to time—moments when they help me with the dishes, and I react to them with pure gratitude. I see the flash of joy they experience in a generous act, and I know that with repetition, the lesson will stick.

Why don't some children get this? Why does one child grow up able to give and share or respond to others with gratitude while another grows up stingy and stuck in some egocentric funk? I'm not a psychologist, but I have to think it has to do with what they observe. It's about role models. I do like to think that almost everything is related to eating sufficient fruits and vegetables, but maybe not this one. This one is about who I am as a parent. If my children aren't generous and giving, I need to look inside.

My radio partner, Grant, is a wonderful teacher by example to his children. Grant and his tender and talented wife take their kids to serve others, sometimes at the homeless shelter or sometimes at Grandma's house. They do these things together as a family, and everyone benefits—especially the children. They are bitten by the bug of giving, of generosity of spirit, and it may be one of the most important things those children will ever learn.

I bet you know people at work who have never learned this lesson. They're stuck in the thirteen-year-old's view of the world, seeing everything as boring or irritating. It's the co-worker who gets called in over the weekend to work overtime and spends most of Monday morning complaining to everyone who will listen. It's the boss who has to do employee evaluations and takes half of each employee's allotted time complaining about the process. And by the way, what's the employee going to say? "But I love these evaluations. Putting a number figure on my immeasurable contribution makes me feel so good about my job." I've heard it said that one negative employee can pull down ten positive ones much faster than a positive one can pull a group of negative ones up. But either way, attitude is infectious.

We know this—we just don't think about it. We don't think about the impact we have on each other. When we go to work with an attitude like Gay, our stellar receptionist, we lift everyone we encounter, even if imperceptibly. And when we complain endlessly about our boss or a slight we feel has been dealt to us by a co-worker, we infect everyone with our irritation and resentment. Just as surely as if we pumped an irritant into the air and they started rubbing their eyes, our spirit has infected them with a sense of picky entitlement and complaint.

I'm not sure when I started to think about this consciously. I think it may have been when I received a letter from a listener of the radio station years ago who told me that without me, she wasn't sure if she could get up in the morning. I know. It sounds like hyperbole, but for this dear woman, I was her lifeline, and I didn't even know her. She was suffering, as I remember it, with cancer. The cancer was not only painful and destructive to her body, it was torturing her spirit. When she would awake, her first awareness was pain. And then she would hear my voice on the radio. She would hear me just reading the news or maybe laughing at my own stupidity, and it felt like salve.

She honored me so much when she wrote me that letter. She honored me, and she taught me in a profound way the effect I have on other people. Suddenly it was more than just talking on the radio. It was more than traffic and weather together every 10 minutes on the 9s. It was life and spirit, and what I did mattered.

I started to check my spirit before I'd go on the air in the morning. How am I doing? If I'm down or grumpy or bitter, that's going to come through the radio. I imagined it infecting people in the shower or driving in their cars, much like that virus infected people in the movie *Outbreak*. Remember that? A little germ would come out of one person laughing in the theater, fly through the air, and enter the mouth of an unsuspecting person three rows back. That germ was just like my spirit. Coming out of me, traveling through the microphone and into the air, being dispensed through the car stereo speaker and unconsciously ingested by the person driving her kids to school, my attitude begins making her anxious and annoyed. And she hasn't the foggiest idea why. It's me. She doesn't know it's me, but it's me . . . I'm infecting her with my grumpy spirit.

I can't let that happen. Even during the most difficult times in my life, I've said a little prayer as I'm driving to work in the morning. And I do it because that dear woman took a moment from her

39

suffering to thank me. "Lord, please help me today. Help me say something that comforts someone. Help me let someone know that he's not alone, that in the midst of his divorce or his financial troubles or other tragedy, there is someone who is with him—if only in this impersonal form of the media. Help me be a friend." That may sound corny to you. That's probably because it is. Some of the best things are.

I want to be the employee who makes you smile when you enter the store, the insurance person on the phone who walks you through the difficult prescription question rather than unfeelingly transferring you into oblivion. I feel so grateful whenever I encounter an employee with this spirit. They just don't know how they lift people. I was in the grocery store the other day and the checker was so helpful. He made fun of himself for not knowing the difference between garlic and shallots, laughed when he couldn't remember the code for Swiss chard (how impressed are you that I'm buying Swiss chard?), didn't shake his head when my toddler starting screaming when I wouldn't let him empty the impulse-buy shelf. I wanted to hug him (the checker, not my toddler). I felt so tired and so ready for the day to be over, and then there he was. He was a literal godsend.

I did the greatest thing the other day in a similar situation. I did it purely by accident, but the response was so unexpected that I want to try to do it as often as I can in the future. I was in the grocery store again (food is probably a little more important to me than it should be), and the checker seemed just frazzled. She was pregnant, about six months from the look of it. Her face was tired, and the man in front of me in line had coupons and complaints and questions. She knew it was taking a long time and that her line, and everybody else's, was getting longer and longer. I did have the fleeting thought: *Why do I always pick the slowest line? Is there something in me that magnetically draws me to whichever line will stop for a price check, a change of cashiers, or a coupon issue?*

And then I had a moment of clarity, of good spirit, as my turn arrived and she began checking me out.

"Sorry about the wait," she apologized.

"No problem at all. I'm not in any hurry," I replied.

This little, insignificant comment produced a look on that cashier's face that I won't soon forget. She almost looked as though she was going to cry. I'm sure some of that was pregnancy hormones (I can say that because I'm pregnant as I'm writing this, and I may start crying at any moment if that telephone doesn't stop ringing), but some of it was the sweetest, simplest relief I've witnessed. I'll bet it had been quite some time since someone had told her to take her time.

As I thought about it more, I realized how rare that comment is. "Take all the time you need. I'm not in a hurry." Most people, including me, are usually in a frantic hurry. That's why we tap our foot in the checkout line, breathe heavily so everyone can hear, roll our eyes, and make other noises that indicate someone is taking entirely too long. That's why we cut in front of people in traffic and run yellow lights. We are in such a hurry. Unless we're complaining, of course, and then we have all day.

I do consciously try to say "take your time" more often now. I do it for the gift of relief it brings. And I do it because it feels really good to give something so appreciated that doesn't cost me a cent. It's the same gift we can give our husbands when they walk in the door late from work. I remember when my husband would often get stuck at work for an hour or more past when he wanted to leave. When he finally got home, his face would look heavy with the sadness of having to be away from his family and with the worry that dinner had been on the stove so long. And when I had the right spirit, I would say, "Don't give it another thought, honey. I'm just glad you're home." And then I'd watch his face lighten right before my eyes.

Try it. Just try it once next time you're in 7-Eleven or next time somebody fouls up and feels bad about it. Let them off the hook. Try giving them the gift of nonjudgment. Try giving them the gift of spirit. Imagine the difference between doing the dishes with your teenager standing around not helping you and doing the dishes with Matthew McConaughey standing around not helping you. If Matthew McConaughey is standing around in his denim, looking fine in your kitchen, suddenly you don't mind one bit that nobody is helping you. You're all about taking care of whatever needs taking care of. "Can I get you anything else, Matt?" Or maybe you work at a convenience store and you wish that the manager would come out of his cave in the back room and help you when you get a rush of people stopping in the store. Now, imagine that one of those people coming in the store is Pamela Anderson. Suddenly you could care less about whether your manager comes out to help. Let him stay in the back. You are suddenly Mr. Customer Service. You can handle it, no problem.

What's the difference? Did your work change? No. The actual work you're doing is identical. What changed was your spirit in response to a powerful outside influence. But that outside influence will never, never be as powerful as what's inside you—and it sure is less predictable. You just can't count on Matthew McConaughey being available to hang out in your kitchen after dinner. But you can count on being able to conjure the spirit of enjoying your work, of taking pride in it, of loving to serve people.

So, Angelina Jolie is in your lobby. Get out there and make some magic.

CHAPTER FOUR

The Volunteer Spirit

"Do not hire a man who does your work for money, but him who does it for love of it."

—Henry David Thoreau

I know some of you are going to fight me on this, but it's worth the fight. Just go with me for a moment. No matter what you're doing in life, you volunteered. There are no slaves in this country, with a few—I'm sure—tragic and rare exceptions. You have choices. If you chose to be a husband, you signed up to be patient and supportive. If you chose to be a mother, you volunteered to clean up catapulted applesauce containers and messy diapers. If you chose to work at the phone company, you signed up to take calls from customers for eight hours a day and help them as much as you can. Whatever job you have, you volunteered. You applied for the job. You accepted the job. And when you did, you agreed to have some hard days, maybe many hard days, until you change your mind and volunteer for another job.

I know this will be hard to swallow for some of you. I'm thinking now of the single mother whose husband left her with no financial support and children to care for. I can hear you. "I didn't volunteer for *this!* I have to work my fingers to the bone, and I still can't take care of my children the way I want to. I didn't volunteer to be abandoned with all these responsibilities." Let me say this first. I'm so sorry. I can only imagine the pain of that circumstance. But what I do know is this—you can't control what you can't control. You can only control what you bring to it. You wanted these children. You were blessed with them. Now—love them as best you can every day with all the spirit you can muster. That's the job you signed up for, whether your husband dies or leaves or stays and actually helps with the laundry. The job is mother now, not wife and mother. Only mother—which is the most important job in the world. Are you going to neglect it and not do your best because you lost the job of wife? You still have the best one.

And I hear you say, "How can I be a mother when I also have to be a breadwinner? When would you suggest I mother, after I work ten hours and sleep six every day?" My answer is: all the while and every chance you get. You can't control what you can't control. If you are diagnosed with multiple sclerosis tomorrow, you will still be a mother. If you win the lottery tomorrow, you will still be a mother. Will you love your children less on the one day than the other? No. You won't. You'll love your children as much every day no matter whether the waitress spills salad dressing on you or your boss fires you or you get a speeding ticket. You'll love your children because that is who you are. The only thing I'm arguing is that you can do it with the volunteer spirit or you can do it with the slave spirit. Which is it going to be? Just remember, your children are going to be affected so much by your choice.

I see the volunteer spirit in the parents of a daughter with Down's syndrome who bring her to Special Olympics bowling practice two nights a week no matter what else is on their plate. They love seeing their daughter excel at something, be with friends, enjoy being alive. They volunteer to coach. They work the registration table at the spring and fall games. You couldn't talk them out of what they do. They love it, and it's obvious. They don't get paid one cent, but they are richly compensated. I suspect they feel more alive while they're doing this work than perhaps anything else they do. This is the spirit I'm talking about, and it's available to you every day in everything you do.

It's the spirit of the formerly homeless man who now spends his Saturdays handing out food at the food pantry and counseling with other homeless men and families. His passion and dedication for his work is clear to everyone he encounters, but not everyone knows why. Most people think he's just an awesome guy and have no idea what he's been through. They don't know that he understands their plight as only someone who's stood in their shoes can. They don't know, and they don't need to know. They feel his spirit and they are lifted by it.

I have a sneaking suspicion that this man does not turn off his volunteer spirit when he goes home or when he goes to his weekday job. He doesn't reserve his passion and engagement only for his work with the homeless, although his heart is tied to that endeavor more personally. He brings the spirit of volunteerism to everything he does. And so can you.

It just requires cleaning your lens. There's nothing wrong with the film in your camera. Nothing wrong with the life you're trying to take a picture of. You just have goop on your lens, and you need to clean it off. Take out the lens cloth and gently rub the specks of dust and dirt off. Remind yourself that this is the life you chose, that you are living your dream right now—until you have another dream—and then you'll live that one. But for now, your dream involves this job, these kids, this car, this dirty carpet, and this weedy garden. This is your current dream. And if you ever change it, then your picture will change too. But for now—let's just concentrate on cleaning the lens.

Imagine bringing the spirit of the volunteer to your life, to all facets of your life. Imagine the passion of the parents of the child with spina bifida who are working to find a cure and fund research. Imagine the love and tirelessness of those parents. This spirit is in you. You already bring it out and use it whenever you truly love something. What I don't understand is why you don't bring it out more often.

I've seen the difference between the volunteer and the slave mentality in bosses I've had. Some of the people I've worked for have struggled in their leadership roles, felt threatened by their employees, been resentful of the talented people they managed. I even remember one boss who was so insecure he actually tape-recorded every meeting we had so that no one could ever misquote him. And then I think of the boss I have now, an incredibly powerful and passionate person named Chris, the first female general manager in my station's nearly ninety-year history. Chris has such amazing energy that people know if she's in her office even if the door is closed.

"Is she in?" one co-worker will ask another passing by her office.

"No. I haven't felt her energy yet," someone will reply with a completely straight face, and the employee who was asking will get it.

Chris has such a volunteer spirit in her job leading these radio stations. She comes to work every day because she loves the challenge, loves the stations she manages and what they stand for, and loves learning more about her world. She is fascinated by technology, by educators of all kinds, by energy in all of its forms, by passion. She loves dedication, appreciates effort, opens her door to all of us, encourages us to solve problems ourselves. And as the football player says in *Remember the Titans,* "Attitude reflects leadership"—and our attitudes reflect her leadership.

We love what we do, and who we do it for, at least in part because of Chris. And it will be no surprise to you that she encourages all of us to volunteer for causes that we feel passionately about. She makes a big deal every year about what we do as a company to support United Way. She supports us in donating our time, even some of our company time, to do volunteer work. She gets involved herself, not only with her checkbook but with her sweat and passion. She is never prouder of me, or any of us, than when we put on T-shirts and take kids from Big Brothers Big Sisters to the zoo. Chris has the volunteer spirit.

In my experience, people seem to do things for one of three reasons. They do them out of fear, out of duty, or out of love. I've been prompted to act for each of these reasons at various times in my life, and I think I still fall prey to the first two, but the only one that feeds my soul is number three—love.

When I think about doing things out of fear, I think of boyfriends I was terrified of losing or jobs I was afraid of being fired from. I would show up to work, look over my shoulder, come in on the weekends, hoping my boss would notice. I didn't love what I was doing. I was afraid of not doing it. If you're ever working late and hoping somebody sees you on the way out, check your spirit. If you're working late trying to close an account and you're energized by the possibility of success, rock on! If you're learning how to play golf because you want your boyfriend to like you, check your spirit (and your choice of boyfriends). Not that there's anything wrong with golf. But there is something wrong with playing golf out of fear of losing your boyfriend.

The problem with doing things out of fear is not necessarily the doing of them. It's the impact on your spirit. There's nothing wrong with working late or learning to play golf. There's nothing wrong with running to stay in shape. In fact, on its face it's good for you. The problem is that if you're doing it so your wife doesn't leave you, it's going to lead to resentment. With every step of well-designed sneaker on treadmill, you're building a wall of resentment between you and your wife. There's nothing wrong with ironing your husband's shirts. That's a lovely and helpful thing to do. But if you do it out of fear that he'll yell at you if you don't, you're resenting every spray of starch.

The resentment is the problem, and you can't avoid it. In fact, if you're not sure what your motivation is—check your resentment level. Do you feel resentful of going to work, baking cookies, sharing your accounts with a new seller, filling out paperwork, shopping for healthier olive oil, whatever? If you do, you've probably got some fear motivation going on there somewhere. And this is sustainable only if you sacrifice your spirit, which is a completely unacceptable alternative—and not your only option. Keep reading.

The second form of motivation I see a lot is duty, which may, in fact, be a form of fear. And let me say right up front that I know there is a lot to admire in the person who acts out of duty. The soldier who serves his country out of duty does us all a tremendous service. The mother who cares for her children out of duty helps them to live and grow. The employee who shows up on time out of duty is commendable. I don't mean to diminish the importance of doing our duty, whatever that is for each of us. I just wish for something more for these strong individuals than acting out of duty alone. What I want to suggest is that duty alone, without love, is good but not good enough for God's work.

God's work, the work our soul was born to do, requires something more. It requires love. It requires full engagement. It requires opening the heart to joy and sharing it with others. This is going to look different in every person, but it's joy just the same. That doesn't always mean laughing-out-loud joy. It may be a quiet joy. It may be a steady, slow joy. But it's joy.

Here's how the duty motivation feels different from joy. The man who comes home to his wife, having said no to a woman who flirted with him at a company meeting, is doing the right thing out of duty. But how different does it feel to you as the wife if he comes home to you because you're the one he loves and he doesn't want to be with anyone else? The man who donates to the firemen's fund because he thinks he should versus the man who donates out of a love and respect for what the firemen contribute and sacrifice for his community. The student who reads the chapter out of duty, wanting to be a "good student," and the student who reads the chapter out of curiosity to learn what's there. The soldier who serves because he is afraid his father will be disappointed if he doesn't, versus the soldier who signs up for love of country and freedom and wouldn't be anywhere else. The daughter who calls her mother because she should. After all, it's been too long and it is her birthday. This versus the daughter who calls her mother out of love and a desire to hear the sweet sound of her mama's voice.

These are not distinctions to be dismissed lightly. I know sometimes nobody but you will know whether the motivation is one or the other, but you're the only one who needs to know. This is your soul we're talking about. Doing any kind of work out of fear leads to resentment. Doing anything out of duty alone can lead to the same, but more often it leads to a feeling of being trapped. I *have* to study. I *have* to be faithful to my spouse. I *have* to clean the house. I'm trapped. I don't have a choice. I'm supposed to. I should. I *have* to!

But if you were motivated out of love, it would be an easy decision and one that would result in a very different feeling. It would take you where your soul naturally longs to be. You would do aerobics out of the joy of feeling your body move. You would think about the man you passed at the market yesterday who couldn't walk easily and feel so grateful that your strong body can jump and sweat and move.

Why would you want to do anything because you *should* if instead you could do it because you *love* it? Isn't the choice yours right now? If you've been wondering why ideas are not coming to you at work, check your love quotient. Do you love what you're doing? If you do, chances are those ideas are going to pop into your mind. If love is the highest power, the strongest emotion, then why would we reserve it only for our families and keep it hidden when we're at work in any other capacity? Why wouldn't love be the right motivation for all things worthy of our precious time?

It's like the old question of what would you do if you knew you had only one day to live? It's likely you wouldn't do anything out of fear. No time for that. And I'd venture a guess that you wouldn't act out of duty either. You would act out of love. And if that's true, why isn't that your motivation every day? There are so many things you can love in any given day that you're missing out on the chance to love right now. You could love the feeling of waking up. (Okay—that's a stretch even for me.) You could love the feeling of a morning walk, the hot water in your shower, the feeling of your car starting up. You could love the taste of food, the smile of a co-worker, the satisfaction of running errands. You could love the sound of your wife's voice on the phone, the feel of your children's arms around your neck, the chance to get out of your work clothes. You could love the smell of dinner cooking, the chance to watch a favorite show, the sound of your dog barking at the neighbor kids. And these aren't even the big things.

"Men are that they might have joy" (2 Nephi 2:25). That line has always resonated so strongly with me. I have never felt guilty or self-indulgent for feeling joy. Though some have tried to encourage a little guilt in me here and there, I simply won't accept it. I know that joy is my natural state. I know it in my cells. I know it in my soul. I am living closest to my *raison d'être* when I experience joy in all of its forms. I remember as a young girl watching my father watch a sporting event. Whether it was me in a swim meet or an athlete in an Olympic track and field event or a beautiful pass completion in football, my father would sometimes be literally moved to tears. And it wasn't necessarily because the athlete (sometimes me) he was rooting for won. Sometimes my dad would tear up when I lost, but the reason the tears flowed was because he was so moved by the spirit of competition. I was inspired by his example, inspired to let the life force flow through me without unnecessary editing.

When we feel joy on all levels, we cry easily. We smile easily, laugh easily, run to a loved one easily. We work easily, share easily, praise each other easily. My challenge to you is to lift the spirit of your work from duty to joy, from requirement to rejoicing. When you do, which could be today if you choose, you will watch not only your own life but the lives of those around you change. It is inevitable. The lens will have been so cleansed that the picture cannot help but be clearer for everyone who looks at it.

When you make this change, and I hope you will, people around you may resist initially. Your wife may chide you, "What are you so happy about?" Your co-workers may razz you, "Who spiked your Wheaties?" Your detractors may deride you, "He's so shallow. Nobody can be that happy all the time." Don't worry. They just don't get it yet, but they will. I think this is one of those things that none of us misses in the end. I have faith that the capacity to experience joy is so deeply embedded in our natures that we will come back to it at some point. I just wish for that to be sooner rather than later.

My friend Linda Eyre, a writer and speaker and teacher of parents around the world, talks a lot about the importance of teaching children to experience joy. Linda says that we worry so much about our children's IQ, but not enough about their JQ—their joy quotient. When our children are in their earliest years, we buy Baby Einstein and play Mozart and want them to know their ABCs before they learn to feed themselves, but we don't often focus on encouraging them to have joy. Joy is their nature. I want to help my children experience that natural state as early and often as possible. If my children have joy, I have done my job as a parent.

Try picturing all things with a Snickers bar if that helps. Monthly reports with a Snickers. Homework with a Snickers. Driving to see your smallest client in Timbuktu with a Snickers. Try picturing yourself handing out a Snickers to somebody who could really use one. Try picturing everything being as good as a Snickers without the calories (or sometimes with). Every day is Halloween and the candy is always free.

Try that one on for spiritual size and see how it feels.

CHAPTER FIVE

Whatever You Want, Give It Away

"I have enough money to last me the rest of my life, unless I buy something."

—JACKIE MASON

I know a few packrats. There are some in my office who appear to have copies of *The Wall Street Journal* from the 1990s. Then there's the guy in TV downstairs who has more bobble-head dolls on his desk than we have employees in the building. Even my husband, who doesn't qualify as a packrat, has some tendencies in that direction. While there aren't trails in between the stacks in our home, he does still keep a stash of old LPs from the 80s and has a suit hanging in the closet that he hasn't worn since he was twenty-one. (He reminds me as I'm writing this that that is perfectly normal behavior.)

I, on the other hand, am probably not normal on this issue. If I haven't used or seen an item for a year, I give it or throw it away. The only things that are not jettisoned under my personal rule of "less is more" are books. Books are sacred, and only a total lack of living space would ever prompt me to part with them. But a perfectly good meat slicer I haven't used? Gone. Mini-muffin baking trays, mixing bowls in various sizes, sets of cheap steak knives? Gone. A winter coat in perfectly good condition that I bought only a year ago but realized moments after I left the store I didn't like? Gone. In my de-cluttering frenzy, clothes of all kinds belonging to any family member are likely to be bundled up and given to charity. In fact, after my son Ethan was born sixteen months ago and I turned forty-two, I gave away all of his baby things—clothes, toys, brand new pacifiers, infant car seat, little Nike shoes, baby bath thing—everything he couldn't use anymore. I also gave away all of my maternity clothes.

And then I got pregnant again. Hmm.

My lack of attachment to things or my need to reduce the number of objects I possess is probably something I should seek counseling for. There must be a happy medium between me and the packrat whose freedom is restricted because she can't get around all of her stuff. I can't explain the payoff for keeping things because I don't understand it, but I can tell you what it feels like to de-clutter. It feels divine! It feels so good to let go, to share with others things I'm not using, to clear and clean and make way. It feels liberating, as though I have everything I need right here and now. I don't need six TVs and a drawer full of jewelry and more than two pairs of black shoes. I don't need twenty turtleneck sweaters or dozens of unused wicker baskets. I just don't need thirteen tubes of sample hand cream or old cans of artichoke hearts I meant to use in a recipe a few years ago.

I love throwing out old magazines, going through my pantry and tossing stale tortilla chips and old Saltine cracker boxes, discarding unused utensils from my junk drawer. I like giving things away that are lovely but that I'll never use—nice pen and pencil sets, colorful watches, decorative stamps, shirts of all kinds with the logos of various companies on them, boxes of milk chocolates. (I'm a picky chocolate eater—it's dark or nothing!) I love dusting the shelves in my laundry room after I've de-cluttered them, love the room created for my hangers after I've removed a dozen items from the closet, love knowing what's actually in my junk drawer.

I can hear my husband protest. "What if you need that some-day?" Yes, he makes a good point. I might someday need this item. Someday I may actually want to use the car cell phone charger, even though I've not felt the need to use it for all of the years I've owned a cell phone. Or someday, big thick leather belts may come back in style. (Oh, shoot—they already have, haven't they?) The answer is, "So?" I don't worry about needing these things someday, not because it's incredibly likely that I won't, but because if I truly need something—I can go get it. But come on—who ever really needs a wood-base pen and pencil set with someone's company logo on it? (Not that there's anything wrong with those—and thank you to all of you who have shared those sets with me in the past.)

The point I'm trying awkwardly to get to is that no matter which end of the packrat scale you fall on, there is something we all need to learn to give away. And I know this is going to sound strange to those of you who are not familiar with this concept. Whatever you truly want, you must give away. This is a law of the universe as I understand it. I don't know why. I just know that since it was intro-duced to me years ago, I have seen it work in every area of my life and in other people's lives.

This is how it works: If you want love, you must love people. If you want respect, you must respect them. If you want support, you must support people. If you want patience, you must be patient with them. If you want money, you must learn to be generous. This is the simple truth of it. Whatever you want, you must give it away.

We all know people who desperately want to be loved. These people may be single and wanting to be loved by a significant other. They may be mothers yearning to be loved by their children. They may be teenagers wanting to be loved, even just noticed, by their parents (for something other than being late). I have the same advice for all of them. Love people. Listen to them. Find ways to love them, whoever is around you, and the love will come back to you. You won't be able to keep it away. If you feel an absence of love in your life, there is only one person to blame—you. (Although blame isn't helpful here.) It's just—you're the only one who can fix it. And you can fix it today.

If you feel disrespected at work, and most of us do at least some of the time, then take a look at your own feelings and behaviors and see who you're not respecting. Do you respect what your boss goes through? Do you respect the pressures on him, the difficult relationships he's juggling, the long hours he's putting in, the expectations he deals with from his superiors? If your co-workers aren't respecting your contribution, look and see if you're respecting theirs. Do you notice your colleague's good work and mention it to him? "Hey, Todd, that was a great deal you closed with a difficult client! No one has been able to close him—and you did it. Way to go! Hope I have a month like you."

If you're a mom who's been wondering why your children never appreciate you, ask yourself when the last time was that you showed appreciation for them. When was the last time you sat down next to your son and told him how much you enjoy being his mom, getting to watch him grow and learn, seeing him play with his brothers? Show him appreciation and you show him how to appreciate. It's like the famous line about how there are only three ways to teach anyone anything—example, example, example. Thank your daughter for helping you with the baby. Thank your husband for mowing the grass and helping to get the kids ready. Thank your wife for making such a delicious meal. Thank them and watch the sense of appreciation grow in your own heart—even before they or others actually begin to return this gift to you.

I'm not sure why this is true—that the only way to fix your world is to fix yourself—but I know that it is. I've discovered that every time I've been frustrated by another person's behavior, it's really me I've been frustrated with! Now that I understand this principle, whenever I even start to think, *Ya know—my son should really respect me more,* I laugh, because I know the truth is that *I* should start to respect more—respect him, respect me, respect others. If I begin thinking that I've been wronged, that someone said or did something to me that they shouldn't, the truth eventually comes. Nope—it's me. I shouldn't have done something. I shouldn't have treated someone carelessly or cruelly.

I think I need to remind myself of this lesson as much as any of you need to hear it. I wonder how many years—years!—of my life I've spent wanting someone else to change. First it was wanting my siblings or parents to change, then wanting a boyfriend to change, then wanting a teacher or professor or boss to change, then wanting a husband to change, then wanting my kids to change, and then still wanting my parents to change. It's never-ending, and it is the source of more frustration in the people I know and talk to than any other single topic.

I think of the endless discussions with my husband where I have complained about a co-worker or a friend or relative, with the underlying thought being, *I wish they were different.* What a fruitless, destructive waste of time that's been. I know better. I know that I can't make anyone change—ever. None of us can. You can't compel your boss to respect you or your kids to appreciate you or your husband to cherish you. The only thing you can do is respect and love and cherish them.

And miraculously—that's all we *need* to do. When I address the problem in me, my world changes. I'm not sure if the other person actually changes, but it sure feels as though they do. Suddenly when I start respecting my boss, I begin to see all of the good things that he does and all of the challenges he faces. When I begin to appreciate my kids, I see them for the beautiful human beings they are, just trying to make their way and figure out who they are. And when I begin to cherish my husband, well, that's the best one of all. When I cherish him, the whole world turns bright no matter what else is happening.

Other than for my family, I am probably the most grateful for my radio partner, Grant. We've been on the air together for coming up on fifteen years. I probably spend more time with him in any given day than I do with my husband. Grant and I have one of those unique friendships where we are endlessly forgiving and fiercely protective of each other. I've always thought we must have been brother and sister in another life. But in addition to the natural chemistry, we also do so many little things to keep our friendship running smooth.

For instance, we buy each other sodas in the morning.

"I say, Amanda," Grant will intone in that deep "I'm a radio announcer" voice.

"Yes," I'll reply, knowing what's coming next before he says a word.

"May I buy you a cold beverage?" he'll inquire with raised eyebrows.

"Why, yes. That would be lovely," I answer in my best Daisy Buchanan voice from *The Great Gatsby*.

We laugh every day, Grant and I, and with any luck we help people to laugh with us. We make fun of our mistakes, never of each other's. We say things to each other like, "You big stud!" or "Thank God for you" nearly every day. Sometimes when our microphones are on and we can't speak out loud, I will point at Grant with my right hand, then point up, down, right and left, then back at him again with emphasis. It's a hand signal that only we know—and it means, "North, south, east, and west—YOU'RE THE BEST!!!!!" Silly? I know. Ridiculous. What was I thinking? That I see him, I support him, and I think he's great. And here's the thing. The more I help him to feel terrific, competent, talented, insightful, creative, and all-around fabulous—the more I feel those things too. In truth, I may be doing it for entirely selfish reasons. It may have nothing to do with Grant. But either way, it's all good.

Giving to Grant in this way, or to Naoma, the receptionist I sing to, or to anyone else costs me absolutely nothing. I was in Costco the other day buying some pre-made chicken burritos and meat enchiladas for dinner. My kids love them and they don't seem to mind one bit that I didn't make them myself (unless I don't microwave them long enough and they're still cold in the middle). As I put the third container in my cart, I looked up into the eyes of a woman behind the glass who was putting the burritos with salsa and sour cream into the containers. She had a hairnet on and wore protective gloves. It was 5:00 P.M., and she looked as though she had worked a long day. I mouthed the words *Thank you* to her. She smiled so big and got a sweet sadness in her eyes. I truly did want to thank her—thank her for spending all day making burritos so I didn't have to. Thank her for putting the chicken and corn and black beans inside and lots of cheddar on the outside. Thank her for helping me make it through this day, all for $2.99 a pound.

That moment with the Costco woman blessed my heart so much. I helped her feel better about her job, if only for a second, and in doing so I blessed myself and my family. I went home feeling more grateful for the food and for my ability to pay for the food. And all this good feeling cost me absolutely nothing. I didn't need to make more money at my job to feel better. I didn't need to put out a memo or schedule a meeting or check e-mail. I didn't need to be thinner or have a smaller nose. I didn't need my kids to make their beds to feel better. I didn't need a manicure or a massage to feel better (although those things would be nice). I instantly felt better from a single thank you, and the glow lasted all night.

This is it. This is the magic elixir that will give you everything you've ever wanted in life. (I guess that's a little grandiose.) Whatever you want, give it away. Lift someone else, and you are lifted. Help your child to feel better about himself, and you will necessarily feel better about yourself as a father and a human being. Help your boss to feel more confident by indicating his contribution is not going unnoticed, and you will go to work with less dread the next day.

I heard a woman speak once who was so powerful. Her name was Rita Davenport, and I believe she was the president of Arbonne International. She understood this principle well. She said, "Learn to be generous, and you'll have more money than your spouse could ever spend," and we all laughed. But I thought a lot about what she said at the time, and I think about it even more now. Money was never that important to me in my twenties and thirties. I liked it, of course. I enjoyed buying clothes and shoes as much as the next girl, but I didn't spend a lot of time thinking about money. I simply spent whatever I made and that was about it. Until I had children. Now I think about money all the time. Will I have enough to help them go to college? Will I be able to pay for their braces and contacts and minor surgeries? Will I be able to pay for their clothes and school fees and calculators? And then there are the little ones. Will I be able to pay for it if they have a major health crisis? What will college cost by the time they get there? Heaven help me.

As I've found myself more concerned about money in recent years, the wisdom of what Rita said and what I've heard echoed from so many other brilliant writers and speakers, is that the sure way, if there is one, to be wealthy is to be generous. And I've found it to be true on at least one and sometimes both of two levels. First, people who give away a portion of their income to those in need, no matter how much that is, are blessed financially. I'm not sure why this is, but my guess is that somehow in their giving they tell the universe that they have more than enough, and then the universe makes it true. The second way in which those who give are blessed is that they are blessed with abundance in all its forms, financially and otherwise. These generous people live with less want, probably with less need, because they focus on the needs of others. It is the magical law that says when you give, you receive. You could not make it otherwise even if you were to try.

So—let's do a little inventory. What do you want right now? I'll answer the question for myself and see if that helps get you started. I want more sleep. (Well, that one I may just have to live with.) I want my husband to be happy. (Then I should be happy.) I want my boss to be pleased with my work. (Then I should be pleased with my work, and with his.) I want my children to be healthy and well-balanced. (Then I should be healthy and well-balanced.) See how easy this is?

So, let the giving away begin!

CHAPTER SIX

What Goes Around

"The weak can never forgive. Forgiveness is the attribute of the strong."
—MAHATMA GANDHI

I'm not proud of it, but I've been a person who has judged another person unfairly. I've held a grudge. I've laughed at someone else's expense (although this one not for a very long time now). I've cut someone off in traffic, and I've tailgated to keep them from merging. I've resented what I'm sure were the good intentions of a friend. And in each of these cases, I've learned the lesson again—what goes around truly does come around.

One of the things I've not been able to figure out in life is why we as a species haven't learned this lesson once and for all, instead of having to relearn it again and again as I do. We learned to refrigerate meat and wear motorcycle helmets and deice planes. Why can't we learn to stop killing ourselves with resentment? Every time we put negativity out there, fill our own hearts and conversations with judgment and ridicule, it hurts us. It may hurt other people, too, but it definitely hurts us. We begin to eat and sleep resentment. We can't get away from it. It haunts our dreams and our relationships with our children. It distracts us at work and takes the pleasure out of everything (except maybe ice cream). It's so destructive and so personally painful, the same as touching our fingers to a hot burner. How could we not have learned to keep our hand away? Why do we still do it? What is the payoff?

I'm not sure. I know it has something to do with fear, but I'm not sure. I think we're so afraid of not being loved or of being hurt, that we bring it on ourselves. I've heard it said that that which we fear, we draw to us. If we fear losing our job, we do. If we fear losing the game once we're up by a touchdown and start playing not to lose—we do just that. If we fear our spouse leaving us, she does. If we fear becoming bitter and rigid, we become just that. I don't know whether the fear points us toward a lesson we are meant to learn or what the universal truth is here, but I see it often enough in myself and the people around me that I know there is truth in there somewhere.

Every hard feeling I've ever indulged in, including the ones that have stuck around for months or even years, I've let go of— eventually. I think that is a big part of the reason why I am healthy. I'm searching my heart right now to see if there are any cobwebbed hard feelings in there still diminishing my life. Let's see. There was this boy who dumped me in high school who never deserved me in the first place named . . . well . . . I guess it would be indiscreet to say his name (Ben Schultz). When I picture him even now I get just a twang of pain. How ridiculous is that? It's been nearly thirty years, and I still feel dumped. Now, do you think Ben Schultz ever interrupts his day to think, *I wonder how that Amanda Dickson is doing? Wonder if she's okay and has gotten over our breakup all those years ago?* Of course he doesn't. He hasn't given it a second thought since 1981. But I hurt myself over and over again all these years later because I can't let go of the resentment. This is not his fault. This is mine. My fault. My choice. My pain.

And when I think about it, I cloud my lens. When I focus on a wrong done to me, however egregious or petty, I hurt myself. The person who supposedly did this wrong to me (which is probably a shaky assumption at best) doesn't suffer one little bit. It's all me. I live in negativity. I wallow in it. It is my food and my oxygen, but with no nourishing value. When I focus on resentment, I dampen the natural enthusiasm of my life. I love the origin of the word *enthusiasm—en theos*—to have God within. When you allow your natural enthusiasm for life to express itself, you have God within. The power of enthusiasm is a divine power.

As is the healing power of forgiveness. (In fact, perhaps they are the same power.) I was moved recently by an example of forgiveness so pure and immediate it humbled me. It brought sudden, stinging tears to my eyes and inspired me to live better. You may remember the story of the Amish children in Lancaster County, Pennsylvania, who were taken hostage by a man who intended to molest and kill them. He did not molest them, but he did shoot all of them and then himself. Many of them died. The pure evil of what he did was horrific on every level and shocked the world. That something so horrible could happen anywhere was heartbreaking. That it could happen in a one-room schoolhouse to the simple and kind Amish people was incomprehensible.

It wasn't two days after this tragedy that the Amish community, including grieving family members, publicly forgave the man who ripped their daughters from them. I remember seeing the grandfather of one of the victims on the news. The reporter asked him, "Are you angry with the man who did this?"

"No," the older man replied.

"Have you forgiven him?" she questioned.

"Yes," he said slowly but without hesitation.

"How is that possible?" the reporter asked, seeming truly incredulous.

"With God's help," the grandfather answered.

Yes. With God's help. With God's power we forgive everyone everything, including ourselves. We forgive ourselves for not being perfect, for obsessing about a relationship gone bad, for being consumed by the slight we perceived dealt to us by a co-worker, for being absorbed by our teenager's flip remark and missing all the other beautiful things she does. We forgive, and when we do, we let joy back in.

I'm not sure how I missed this in law school, but it came as something of a shock to me when I started practicing law that the majority of my time would be spent criticizing other people. When I studied case law in school, I studied the arguments other lawyers made, the decisions judges made, the language they used. I studied the heroic belief of civil rights attorneys and the courage of rookie lawyers bringing cases on behalf of the less privileged. I studied property law and criminal law and torts—the law of wrongful acts. Somehow the studying of these situations, all fights really when it comes right down to it, did not trouble my spirit. But being in the fight myself? That was excruciating.

I had all the wrong instincts for a lawyer. I wanted to forgive the other side every time they were late with a filing. "No problem. Next week works great." I wanted to talk my clients out of suing. "I know that you feel hurt, deservedly so, and that you are filled with righteous indignation right now, but go home and live with this feeling for a couple of days. Then call me and tell me if you can stay this dedicated to being mad for five years or more, which is about how long it will take to resolve this. And by the way, you'll never get as much money as you think you should." I wanted to hug people during depositions, began to cry when opposing counsel insinuated I was lying (something I didn't know was a common practice until I got into the law), broke out in hives when another lawyer would say something hurtful to my client just to get a reaction. I was not a good lawyer.

People want their lawyer to be a pit bull. They don't want their lawyer to be sympathetic. I'm not a good pit bull. No matter how much I would believe in my client and his cause, I struggled with spending my days looking for weaknesses in the opponent to exploit. I could not exploit them once I found them. I could not encourage a client to be unforgiving even if it meant I would lose my fee. I couldn't charge him for every minute of every phone conversation we had, especially when we were talking about things in general. I couldn't be on the defensive in every interaction I had with another human being. Now, having said that, I need to tell you that I have tremendous respect for many lawyers I know, including my father—lawyers who are brilliant and dedicated to their clients and to the law. I am glad they are there and can do this hard work. I cannot. The day I gave my month's notice to the law firm, I drove home weeping, wiping tears from my cheeks, belting out "Amazing Grace" as I tried not to cause an accident. "That saved a wretch like meeeeeeeeeeee!"

I could not separate work from home, work from life, work from me. I couldn't do it when I was a lawyer, and I can't do it now. What I do for a living is who I am, a big part of who I am, and I couldn't be a fighter for a living. Toward the end of my third and final year in the practice of law, I found myself starting to turn my newly developed skill of interrogation and criticism on the people I loved. As I learned to pick apart everything anyone ever said, I turned it on my husband. Suddenly, every opinion he expressed, every tidbit he shared with me from something he read, I would cross-examine.

"Now, you say that as if you have personal knowledge, but you don't," I would argue.

"I'm just saying I heard on the news that it's going to rain." He looked a little stunned as he walked off to the kitchen.

Or . . .

"Want to go out for an ice cream?" my husband would ask.

"Sure," I'd reply.

Later at Baskin Robbins, he would order a double cone of something, often something with chocolate or macadamia nuts.

"Have you considered all your options?" I'd question.

"This is good," he'd mutter through licking the cone.

"Yes, but did you consider all your options? Did you weigh them? Did you see the double chocolate fudge over here? Did you consider your sundae options?" I was relentless.

The counter attendant would get frustrated and help someone else.

My life suffered because I turned this criticism, this nitpicky cross examination, on my husband. My marriage suffered. And my husband wasn't the only victim. I needled my friends, my family, everyone I came into contact with, including myself. I second-guessed every thought I had, looking to see how it might be exploited later. I worried about everything I wrote or said on the phone. I looked for the bad in others and turned that judgmental eye on myself. I was miserable, and I'm grateful every day that I'm free of it now. I am quite sure that I make a complete fool out of myself far more often now, either on the air or in a speech I'm giving or at the grocery store. I may even say things I might later regret.

But I hardly ever think to criticize anyone anymore. The desire to scrutinize just doesn't occur to me.

In fact, the exact skill I was paid to master at the law firm would likely lead to me getting fired in nearly any other job. Criticism and negativity. I think the easiest way to get fired, if that is your goal, is to be a downer at work. Complain about your pay. Complain about your boss, your hours, your co-workers, your wife. Complain about your car, your finances, your commute, the quality of your latte—whatever. If you are one of those people who sucks the life out of every room you're in, they will find a way to fire you. (Or at least I would if I were your boss.) And this result would not be due to any lack of talent or ability on your part. It is entirely due to your attitude and the impact your attitude has on the workplace.

I worked with a guy some years ago who was a perfect example of this principle. He got hired at the station, and the complaining began almost immediately. I watched him do many things well, even excel in some areas, and I watched the station give him an incredible opportunity—some would say a once in a lifetime opportunity—to really make a name for himself. He complained before he got the promotion. He complained while he worked in his new capacity. And he complained about everything and everyone. He didn't like having to meet with clients. He didn't like having to attend lunches for the children's hospital. He didn't like how he perceived other people got more attention than he did.

I remember he asked me once with an adolescent scowl on his face, "How come you get to do everything you want to do?" I looked at him a little sideways while I thought for a minute. First of all, it was a ridiculous question. Of course I didn't get to do everything I wanted to do. I'd been asking the station to send me to Paris for years so I could do the show live from a sidewalk cafe and report on the magnificent women in hats, but they never went for it. I couldn't even get a week in Hawaii for a special broadcast on the healing power of swimming with dolphins.

But let's assume for a minute that I get to do a number of things.

I replied, "Maybe it's because people don't mind being around me." I raised my eyebrows to help with the meaning, but he just muttered something derogatory and shuffled away. I thought about how poor his posture was. And I wondered what it would take to help him have joy in his work. I wanted to help him. I hated seeing him suffer, stuck in this loop of negativity, unable to see how good he had it. He had so much talent. He was in a beautiful place. I thought if I told him stories about the law firm, about how hard he could have to work for a living, about what real jobs looked like, he might start to appreciate what he had and then enjoy it.

It didn't work. He got fired. And although many of us felt sad, none of us was surprised. He got fired because he could find no joy in anything, including his job. He got fired because he pointed out the negative in every situation. He got fired because that is exactly what he needed. He just didn't know it.

I'm not sure if he knows it yet. I remember after he got fired, he kept asking "Why?" He asked his supervisor why. The answer was unacceptable to him. He asked the general manager why. The GM deferred to personnel. He asked personnel why, and they deferred to his supervisor. He asked me why, and I didn't have the strength to tell him the truth: "It's because of you. You got fired because you drained the energy and passion from everyone you encountered, and no business can afford that kind of loss of resources." I think the best I could come up with that day was, "It may not have been fair, but if you really want to know the answer—you've got to look inside." I don't think he heard me.

Have you worked with a person such as this? If you have, I'll bet his or her name is right there. You just said it aloud, didn't you? They're memorable, these unhappy people. I think most of us have worked with at least one perpetually disgruntled person in our careers. If you haven't worked with someone like this, that's rare. I think there has been at least one in every one of my jobs. There was a waitress at the steak house who griped all the time and wondered why she never got any shifts. There was a model in the modeling agency I worked for who complained about the clothes and the pay and wondered why she never got any shows. There was a teacher at the university who wanted to be full-time, but complained so much about being part-time that he lost the classes he did teach. See?

I have to catch myself, too. Once in a while I get stuck in this loop, in this funky, dissatisfied place of seeing everything wrong outside me. I roll my eyes a lot when I'm in this place. I look for other people's mistakes so I can say, "See? See how he screws up?" I sigh a lot, breathe heavily, walk slowly. I get frustrated constantly and by little things. Stapler out of staples? That will send me into the ozone. Boss doesn't return my call as fast as I think he should? I need to teach that guy a lesson.

Which reminds me. A big part of the negative loop is physical. The sighing, the heavy breathing, the eye rolling, the hunched shoulders, the shuffling gait. I have noticed in my life that it's hard to maintain a good quality depression if I look like Goldie Hawn. And I'm not talking about petite and blonde and beautiful. I'm talking about animated, where every muscle of your face is alive and aware, where your body is alert and dancing. If you look like that, you will likely begin to laugh, to find something to laugh at, to see some joy somewhere because your body is positioning you to see it. That kind of energy attracts joy to it—moth to a flame. Goldie is irresistible, and so are you when you have that joy emanating from your skin.

This is likely not a new concept for you. You've probably heard many people use the phrase "act as if" in some form. Act as if you are happy, and you are. Act as if you're patient, and you are. Act as if you're a great mom, and you are. When you pretend to be a jogger by jogging, you, in fact, become a jogger. Maybe not a good one, maybe a reluctant one, but a jogger still. And I know there are a lot of deeper questions here as to what and who the soul really is, about what is genuine, about what in the heart is trying to express itself. But here's the thing. How we feel is a matter of choice. With some medical exceptions, it is a choice. If you want to be a better mother, choose to be such. Begin acting as if you are today. Wake up before your kids do. Make breakfast. Make their lunches. Take advantage of teaching moments. Care about what's in their back-packs. When they leave, do some cleaning. Write in your journal. Plan dinner. Do the things you think good moms do, and you become a good mom.

When you pretend to be happy, open your face and your eyes, and start truly listening to your spouse or your boss, your spirit comes along. At least in my own experience, my spirit follows my body and my actions. I remember during the saddest times of my life, times when what I was enduring emotionally felt as if it would squeeze all the oxygen from my lungs, I would sometimes have to go out in public for some reason. Sometimes it was to perform in some way where I needed to appear happy and engaged, or at least not psychotic and tortured. Sometimes I just needed to go to the grocery store or the dry cleaners. I would sit in the car before going into wherever, and I would smile the biggest, dumbest smile I could while looking in the rearview mirror. I would sometimes do this while tears were streaming down my cheeks, but I would do it. I would do it until I realized how stupid I looked or sometimes until someone walking by would look over at me with that "Are you totally nuts?" expression. And in that moment of humor and humility, the spirit would come. The joy would come. And I would see something to smile about, if only that my mascara miraculously had not been totally ruined.

Now some of you may be saying, "Aren't you encouraging us to fake it? Isn't there something wrong with the dishonesty in pretending? You're being dishonest with yourself, aren't you? And who does that help?" Everyone, is my answer to the last question. Faking it is really just practicing. You're practicing how to be happy so you're ready when you really are. You can either practice how to be depressed and miserable, how to be disheartened and resentful, or you can practice how to be joyful. Either way, you're going to get really good at one of them. It's not likely you will be good at both—each requires too much commitment in time and energy.

I once heard a woman say, "Don't tell people your problems. Half of them don't want to hear it, and the other half think you deserve it." Good advice. Rings true, doesn't it? How many times have you listened to a whining co-worker and gone home that night, recounted the story to your spouse, then added, "Well, what does she expect?" You can't fix the co-worker. We know that for sure. But we should look inside on this one. Does anyone dread seeing you walk through the door? Let's start where it really counts. Does your spouse dread seeing you walk through the door? Do you begin to complain and point out fault the minute you open the door or the minute she walks into the room? Do you sense that you have a profound effect on that person's mood? Does your husband walk in happy, hugging the kids, and quickly get heavy from being around you?

Or your kids. Let's talk about them. Is the first thing out of your mouth when you see your kids after school, "You WILL clean that room today." Or do you smile at them, hug them, ask them about their day? When your baby starts to cry, do you immediately sigh and say, "Oh, no!" Or do you soothe and smile and tell her everything is going to be all right?

Do your co-workers or employees dread seeing you walk into a room? Can you feel their energy decrease when you approach? Do they smile and become engaged with you? Do you smile and engage with them? Do you show them respect, really listen when they're talking, or are you checking e-mail and making snide comments while they're sharing their ideas?

I think we all know whether or not we are one of these people, and perhaps we all behave like this some of the time. I'm sure there have been times when my spouse or my co-workers have dreaded seeing me. But I'm also sure I'm not that person on a regular basis. I check it, just like I check to make sure my skirt isn't tucked into the back of my pantyhose. I check my spirit. When I'm greeted first thing in the morning by a co-worker, what is my first response to the "How ya doin'?" question? Is it, "Great. Hanging in there. How are you?" Or do I go into my first whine of the day?

And I check it with my spouse. I can tell from the quality of his attention whether I'm starting to burn him out. If I've been complaining about something at work or something with the kids, and I start to sense he's saying "Uh-huh" without really hearing me, I change the subject—or just stop talking altogether. And I don't get mad at *him* when this happens. A person can only take so much. When his energy wanes, it's a cue to me that I'm draining him, which means I'm draining me. Next subject. Hey—how about a walk with the kids today?

What goes around truly does come around. Let this truth be an instructor to you. If you're getting negativity and complaint everywhere you go, it can't be all about "them." It's about you. What's going on in you? Where is the negativity and complaint coming from in you? If your kids and your spouse are avoiding you, coming into the room laughing but then quickly being quieted by your demeanor, there is nothing wrong with them. What's going on in you?

How can you begin to put something more positive out into the world, into your home, into your job? If it requires a little pretending at first, who did that ever hurt? I used to love to play dress-up as a kid. I wasn't hurting anybody, and neither will you be. In fact, you may stop hurting someone.

You.

CHAPTER SEVEN

Handling Criticism

"I don't know the key to success, but the key to failure is trying to please everybody."

—BILL COSBY

Y ou're going along having a perfectly good day until your boss calls you in and says:

"You really missed the mark on that one."

"You need to check with me before you ever have another idea."

"I guess today's performance was not one for the time capsule."

"I do not have time to babysit everything you do."

"I know you disagree with me, but I'm the boss, and I'm not interested in having this conversation with you anymore."

Or you get home in reasonably good spirits and before you can even change your clothes you hear:

"Mom! Why do you always take his side? You never even listen to me."

"So are you ever going to clean out the garage or should I hire someone to do it?"

"Are you still eating donuts at work? Because that weight sure isn't coming off."

"Why aren't you coming, Dad? All the other dads will be there!"

"Are you going to be late getting home every night this week or just tonight?"

And you're done.

You were riding such a good mood, handling little issues that came up during the day, until that mean-spirited word from your boss or your spouse or your teenager, and you're done. You've lost all your joy. You feel ready for battle—or for surrender. Maybe you go into full attack-back mode, pointing out everything wrong with the other person, matching mean comment for mean comment. Or maybe you shut down, become quiet and withdrawn, even stop hearing what the other person is saying. Either way, your spirit is deflated, your enthusiasm lost, your energy kaput.

Some of you deal with this kind of hard criticism every day. I'm so sorry. Maybe you work for the airlines or the Department of Motor Vehicles and people verbally assault you on a regular basis. Maybe you're a teacher or a coach who is criticized by parents every week, even as you try to do the best you can for their children. Maybe you're a stepparent who gives everything you have to children who won't even look at you. I'm sorry. I know it is hard, seemingly impossible at times, to have joy in the face of such joylessness.

But there is a way. It may be difficult to imagine if your job is to write parking tickets or reject people's insurance claims, but there is a way. Even if you spend most of your time doing employee evaluations, there is a way to have more joy in the face of criticism. And may I just say something here about employee evaluations while I'm thinking about them? I've never known anyone who enjoyed getting them—or giving them. I realize it is in the nature of corporations to want to attach a number to intangibles such as individual effort and progress. If companies can't measure something, they panic. How do we evaluate if we can't measure? How do we measure if we can't evaluate?

Some things just don't fit on a sliding scale. Some aspects of the human experience are not reducible to a number. They're just not. And forcing them into a finite tangible does not give you information that is useful. It gives you information—it's just not useful because it's not accurate. Some bosses are reluctant to give perfect scores: "Nobody can be perfect." And some bosses are reluctant to give anything but: "He tries so hard." Neither description is either accurate or relevant. This is why corporate executives love Gallup and similar surveys, but employees hate them. We don't hate them because we're trying to be difficult. We love being asked our opinion, and we benefit from feedback. We just aren't "graphable," so stop trying. Talk to us, and listen to us, and if you need something in the file then take the time to write a paragraph or two.

Whew. Thank you for indulging my rant there. I started to hear Dennis Miller saying, "That's just my opinion. I could be wrong."

Back to handling criticism. I have never known anybody who says they are really good at handling criticism. I've witnessed co-workers and friends handle it better or worse, but I've never met anybody who breezes through it unscathed. Even when the criticizer reminds us not to take it personally, we do. Of course we do. In fact, if anything, we brace ourselves when we hear the preface, "Now don't take this personally . . ." That phrase is usually followed by something like, "but you might want to think about wearing deodorant." Or, "we'd appreciate it if you didn't come talk to us in the future." Or, "I haven't enjoyed a meal you've cooked since the 80s."

No matter the intent, criticism feels personal. Even when the speaker wishes not to inflict any pain, it still hurts. It hurts because what we're hearing is that the way we are is not okay for someone else. Whatever we've been doing, whatever we thought was best or at least acceptable, isn't. Our parenting isn't good enough. Our work isn't good enough. Our body isn't good enough: "Fatty fatty two by four. Can't fit through the kitchen door."

Which is not to say that sometimes we don't benefit from this feedback. Sometimes feedback such as this, even when it's painful, can be life-changing. It can be the push, the nudge, the uncomfortable moment that propels us to do something. Sometimes the cruel comment is just painful enough that our spirit ignites, rebels, and takes a stand. "I am *not* stupid." "I am *not* worthless." "I am *not* a failure. Look at these beautiful, well-adjusted children I'm raising and tell me again that I'm a failure!"

I feel pain when I'm criticized. Even after all the practice I've had. I often get teary even at inappropriate moments, like at work when I'm on the air or in the middle of a meeting. And let me just tell the men reading this book that if a woman in your presence begins to cry in a professional setting, it is not her intention to do so. She did not wake up that morning and think to herself, *Now, let me see, I wonder if it would really help my career if I were to burst out bawling in the middle of this meeting.* The truth is, she is likely digging her fingernails into the palm of her hand to try to stop herself from crying, but it's not working. Crying is a natural, physical function for us—like sweating is for you. Neither is wrong. They just are. Don't read too much into it. Give us a minute and move on.

If you receive a fair amount of criticism in your life, which I would guess many of you do, then let me tell you something. You're in good company. Some of the most talented and successful people I know have gotten knocked off their horse on a regular basis.

When I met talk show host Sean Hannity some years ago, he was emceeing an Independence Day event where my station was a sponsor. He was there with a number of other celebrities, and there were many people crowding around him. Being a little bashful in public situations, I held back. (I know that's hard to believe.) At some point in the dinner before the festivities began, one of Sean's assistants approached me and said, "Mr. Hannity would like to meet you."

I was so flattered. Well, of course. We walked over to where he was shaking hands, and he said, "Are you Amanda Dickson?"

"Yes, I am. What a pleasure to meet you, Mr. Hannity."

"Sean, please. Hey. I wanted to meet you because I'm told you're the only person at KSL who gets more hate mail than me."

Awkward pause.

"Well, yes, that is a distinction I'm not exactly proud of, but yes."

It's true. I do receive quite a bit of what we call hate mail. By that I mean mean-spirited mail that is attacking and sometimes threatening. It's not just a suggestion or constructive criticism. It's biting and proud of itself.

I used to receive this hate mail in hard copy form. I would keep it in a file marked, yes, "Hate Mail." The file got so thick, I had to start a second file. Years ago when we were moving our cubicles into another area of the building, I looked at these two bulging file folders. I even pulled them out and flipped through some of the now years-old letters. Why was I keeping them? So I could refer to them later? So I could remember how much they hurt the first time? Talk about bad feng shui.

I threw them away. How liberating. And then I started getting hate mail in voice mail form, followed by e-mail form.

I remember one voice mail in particular. It had to do with my public address announcer job. One of my eighteen jobs in the last twenty years was being the PA announcer for the Utah Starzz. The Starzz were Salt Lake's WNBA franchise for five years. They were great fun, and I had a thrilling time working those games. For those of you who aren't familiar, the public address announcer is the loud, booming voice you hear in the arena who says things like "Hey—how 'bout those Jazz?" or the less inspiring, "Foul on number 13. And the Bulls will shoot two." It's an adventure to be sitting at mid-court on the floor when loose balls go flying past your head and anxious players wanting to sub into the game come and bang on your table to get your attention. It was also a thrill to feel short for the first time in my life. I am somewhat of an Amazon woman. If I were an alien, I would definitely be Klingon. But when I would stand for the national anthem in WNBA games, I was as short as the point guards. The centers and power forwards towered over me. Ahhh. It felt so good to be petite.

Well, one night I'm leaving the arena and I check my voice mail as I'm driving home, a neurotic habit I still have today. I listened to a message from a guy, and I could tell he had left it for me during the game because I could hear *me* in the background. That was a slightly unsettling experience. Anyway, what he said (edited for all audiences) was "You have no business being a PA announcer. You don't know the first thing about basketball. Was there not a competent woman in the Mountain West who could handle this position? Keep your day job!" Blah. Blah. Blah. You know how the voice mail lets you go on for two minutes and then beep-beeps and cuts you off? He went on for the two whole minutes. (And I listened to the two whole minutes.)

At first I had the instinct to cry, which had been my common response to someone yelling at me—even in voice mail. But I hesitated. And I thought, *Yes!* (I may have even done a Tiger Woods, closed-fist pump at this point.) *I inspired a man to pick up a cell phone in the middle of a basketball game, use his precious minutes to call the maze that is our company voice mail system, find my mailbox, and chew me out good for two whole minutes. There is nothing mediocre about that!*

I was starting to learn something about the nature of mean-spirited criticism. I wasn't quite there yet. I still needed a little more practice, but I was starting to see the light. Just a few weeks ago, I received a hate e-mail while I was on the air. I am, like most women I know and more than a few men, a multitasker. In my job, that means that I have two newspaper Web sites, my newscast, my commercial copy, my e-mail, and probably at least one or two other web pages I'm surfing minimized on my computer while I'm on the air. My supervisor used to label this behavior as distracted or scatter-brained until his supervisor became a woman. She taught him that men and women accomplish tasks differently. Men are linear. They take on a project, kill it, take on another project, kill it, etc. Women, on the other hand, do five projects simultaneously. The men and women actually finish around the same time. One way is not more effective than the other. They're just different, and the difference is gender related.

So on this specific morning I'm thinking of, I received a nasty e-mail halfway through the broadcast. I read it, and even after all these years of practice, I felt the tears coming. Shoot! I was coming back from commercial and couldn't push the tears away in order to talk. I pointed at Grant with that look on my face that said, "Talk. Please! While I get it together." He did. He talked for as long as he could, until finally he said on the air, "You just got a nasty e-mail, didn't you?"

"Yes," I answered, still sniffling. "I'm such a boob. I know better than to let something like this get to me. I'm sorry."

It was a little embarrassing, but somehow, disclosing it helped the pain begin to pass, and just as it did—the e-mails started pouring in. In two minutes' time, I must have received fifteen loving e-mails. They said such things as, "You forward me that nasty e-mail right now this minute. I'm going to let that guy have it. How dare he upset you? You are such a wonderful person!" Oh, the outpouring of affection! It was like being hugged right through the computer. I can't tell you how good it made me feel. So good, in fact, that I wrote back to the guy. I don't usually do this, at least not while I'm upset because I do have the "Mama rule" for e-mail: If Mama can't read the e-mail, I can't send the e-mail. Especially not from my work address.

But I felt so good after receiving all of those supportive e-mails that I did write back. I said:

"First of all, let me just apologize for my energy. I know it can be really annoying, especially at this time of the morning, but I can't fix it. I don't drink too much caffeine. This is just how I am. But here's what I know for sure. Whatever is upsetting you so much that you'd write an e-mail that nasty to a woman you don't even know is not about me. I'm nobody in your life. I'm not your wife or your boss or your neighbor. I'm just some dumb woman on the radio. Change the station!

"What your writing to me this morning tells me is that you're in a pretty scary place right now. And for whatever is causing you this pain, I'm sorry.

"I wish you well."

Then I hit send.

Grant said, "If he writes you back, don't you dare read that while we're on the air." Isn't that cute—how men think they can tell you what to do? Well, the guy did write back. Shocking. Usually people like that don't want to have a dialogue. They want to strike, hopefully inflict pain, and then retreat. They don't want to approach anything reasonable. But this man did. He wrote back:

"Amanda, you're right. I was too hard on you. I just didn't think anybody could genuinely be that enthusiastic. I'm sorry."

Oh, my, gosh! I couldn't believe it. He owned it? He actually owned being unreasonable and hurtful? Nobody does that. What a great guy. I wrote back:

"I can't believe you wrote back. You renew my faith in humanity. What a great guy you are. "

He wrote back:

"And you're a nicer person than I thought."

I let it go right there. I figured if we kept going, we'd be having a date, and considering I'm married and pregnant—that's probably not such a good idea.

Then the truth I had been sensing in flashes here and there came flooding in with full clarity. Mean-spirited criticism gives you no information about you. None. It doesn't teach you anything about your intelligence, your ability, your beauty, the way you do your job, or anything else. It might as well be gibberish. It's as if the communication takes on the quality of Charlie Brown's teacher. Can you hear her? "Blah, blah, blah, blah, blah, blah."

The only thing mean-spirited criticism does tell you is something about the speaker. It tells you the speaker is in a pretty awful place, a place of such spiritual poverty and pain that it actually seems like a good idea to lash out and hurt someone else. And know this—the speaker does not feel better after he or she lashes out at you. It must seem like a good idea to her at the time to take you to task for being late or wearing that jacket or making a mistake, but it does not give her the satisfaction she craves. I know this because I've been the one lashing out.

I'm not proud of it. But I want you to know that I know how bad it feels to be the criticizer. I remember clearly the last time I did it. I remember feeling such frustration, such a wounded ego, that I lashed out at someone I love. I yelled. I accused. I judged. I was filled with self-righteousness and a desire to hurt this person's feelings. It worked. I did make him feel bad, but not as bad as I made me feel. In fact, the more I yelled at him, the worse I felt. It was like a drug you begin to get immune to, so you have to take more and more for the same effect. I couldn't be critical enough, so I kept pushing until I cried. Only the breathlessness of the tears got me to stop.

I remember that I was driving while I had this conversation. Talk about stupid. It's dangerous enough to have a pleasant conversation while whisking down the freeway at 70 miles an hour, but to have an emotionally charged conversation at that speed? How could I have been so irresponsible? I hope the memory of it keeps me from ever doing it again. That day, after I eventually hung up, I started to pray out loud. "Lord, let me forgive—myself and him. Let me forgive him for whatever I feel he did wrong. And help me forgive myself for being so cruel just now. Let me have endless forgiveness. Let me forgive him—and me—again and again and again." My mantra that day as I drove to give a speech was "endless forgiveness." I whispered it over and over again as I pulled into the parking lot.

I wondered how I would ever stop crying long enough to speak to this group—a group of elementary school secretaries from around the state, a lovely group of angels in the office who help our youngest and most vulnerable children every day. I was asked to speak to help get them excited and enthused about life and their jobs—and I had barely stopped crying before I walked in the door. How was I ever going to help them feel enthusiastic while I was in that condition? I waited at the doorway to the conference hall for my turn to go on, and as I waited, the speaker before me was finishing up. She was telling the story of how her husband had gone on a fishing trip three years before. In fact, she had encouraged him to go, to get out and enjoy himself for a change. He had spent so much of the recent years helping her with the endless needs of their four small children.

When the doorbell rang late that night, she thought to herself, "Ahhhh. He's missed me. Isn't that cute? He's missed me and just couldn't stay away. I bet he forgot his keys." She opened the door in her robe with a smile on her face to find two state police officers standing there. They told her that earlier that afternoon, her husband had been struck by lightning, that he had fallen into the stream where he was fishing and drowned.

And her life as she knew it ended right there.

She shared that story with us to leave us with the reminder to enjoy every day, to take the time every day to love our families, to tell them how much they mean to us, to not waste one precious minute. I began to cry again and felt my body go white hot. The man standing next to me asked me if I needed water. "Yes. Thank you," I said and tried to get it together as the woman finished her speech and the host went to the podium to introduce me. As I wiped the tears from my face, again, I took the microphone and told those wonderful secretaries that I knew why I had come that day— and it wasn't to speak to them, although I would do my best. It was to hear that woman share that story, and I thanked them for having me.

I know I'll probably forget this lesson and have to learn it again someday, but I hope it's a long time from now. My prayer today is: "Let me waste no more time criticizing others. Let me waste no more precious energy pointing out their faults, lowering their confidence, sucking all the oxygen out of the room. Let me contribute to laughter, not pain. Let me have endless forgiveness."

So we know now that mean-spirited criticism gives us no information about us, only about the speaker and the dark place he or she is in. I hope you remember that the next time your boss clips your wings or your teenager spits some nasty comment in your direction. When it happens to me now, and it does regularly, I pause and go there. I go to the place of the nasty criticism. I have to go there first because there may be a lesson I need to learn in there somewhere. Did I make a bad judgment call in my job that day or would I do it again exactly the same way? Did I ignore my teenagers' needs or are they just being hormonal? I go there, and then after I decide if there is anything for me to learn, I remember that the tone of their criticism, the arrogance or cruelty, is all about them— not me.

The bummer is that the opposite is also true. We want to think praise is the honest truth, completely based in fact, and so well-deserved because, after all, we are wonderful. But praise likely doesn't give you any substantive information about you either. It also tells you something about the speaker. It tells you the speaker is in a generous place, a place of such abundance that she has plenty to share. Now, you *may* be wonderful, do wonderful things, look fantastic, but these things aren't so because someone pointed them out to you. They were already true.

Either way, though, you're okay. You're okay no matter what someone says to you, says about you, writes to you in an e-mail. It's like this. When someone tells me I'm the most delightful person they've ever met, I understand. And when someone tells me I'm the most irritating person they've ever met, I understand. Either way—it's their opinion. What does it have to do with me? It's their business. Like the title of a book I saw in the store once—*What You Think of Me Is None of My Business.*

Amen.

CHAPTER EIGHT

Get Off the Dead Horse

"Life is an adventure in forgiveness."
—Norman Cousins

How do we get past the pain and humiliation of a dressing down? Whether it's our mother telling us we aren't raising our kids well or our boss telling us in front of our co-workers that we are a great example of what he doesn't want, how do we let go? It sounds so easy, "Let go," like something Jacob Marley would whisper to Ebenezer Scrooge, but how do we do that? How do we walk away from the pain of that and feel lightness in our spirits again? Maybe you'll encounter an angel as I did in the woman who shared the story of the loss of her husband, but you can't count on an angel. We've got to be our own angels.

Several years ago, I heard a woman speak who was talking about what to do when we get stuck, and I would think feeling stung by criticism is a great example of getting stuck. She said, "For those of you who are stuck, I'm going to tell you seven words. You're going to remember them and they're always going to help you. And they are: When—the—horse—is—dead, GET—OFF!"

We roared with laughter. She continued, "But no. We nurturers, we stand over the dead horses of our lives and we say, 'Come on, horsy. You can make it. It's my fault. I didn't buy you the right oats. I didn't buy you the right saddle. C'mon, horsy!' But the horse is dead."

At that moment, a tiny little woman in the back of the room raised her hand bashfully. The speaker said, "Yes?" and the woman asked, "Well, how can you tell if the horse isn't just . . . um . . . comatose?" Oh—we laughed so hard, and when the speaker could finally be heard over the roar, she said, "Hang in there, sweetie, but if you begin to detect a terrific stink, it's dead. GET OFF!"

What are the dead horses in your life? Is there a painful thought that repeats in your head over and over as you're trying to go to sleep? Maybe a conversation with your boss where you felt devalued or disrespected, and it keeps playing in your brain over and over and over? *How could he have said that to me?!* That's a dead horse. Maybe you wake up in the morning and before you're even fully conscious you already think, *Oh, I hope I don't see her at work today. She just drives me completely crazy. She is the most irritating person.* That's a dead horse. Or right after your kids have walked out the door to school, you go around the house muttering to yourself, "How many times have I asked them to clean up this mess? I'm sure they're incubating some disease in this room. It smells awful in here. Why don't they ever do what I say before I have to nag them a hundred times?" That's definitely a dead horse.

And here's the thing about dead horses. It's the same way with forgiveness. You get off the dead horse because it's what *you* need to do. Forget what effect, if any, it will have on any other person. You get off because you're stuck there not going anywhere and the flies are starting to get thick. You get off because you want to keep moving in your own life. You get off because there may be another great horse waiting for you, or your own two legs are doing just fine at moving you along. You get off for you!

Your dismissing boss or irritating co-worker may have a great "aha" moment in his life that will suddenly cause him to see the error of his ways, but your well-being can't wait around for that. Your kids will likely grow up, may even have kids of their own, and someday they may appreciate all of the sacrifice you endured for them, but you can't put your happiness on hold until that day comes either. All of the time we invest in wishing these people, whoever they are, would change is just so much wasted life. It doesn't do the person we're stewing over any good, and it certainly doesn't help us. We might as well take the precious hours and days we spend gritting our teeth and convert that time into hundred-dollar bills, then crumple them up and chuck them in the trash. That is how wasteful our thinking is.

I remember being particularly stuck at one point in my life. A relationship had gone bad, and I felt completely lost without it. I felt that my entire life had been a failure, that there was no hope for me, my career, or my future, that I would never have a family or any of the things I had dreamed of. I couldn't focus at work. I couldn't talk to friends. I could barely stand to be awake. I think the only food I could stomach for weeks at a time was Frosted Flakes.

During this time, I would have stayed in my apartment and stopped showering altogether if I could have. I took baths just so I could cry in a different place, and I never combed my hair afterward, so after a few days, I looked like some MTV grunge rock band creature. If I did try to go out in public, even just to the grocery store, the tears would just come. I remember feeling pathetic in the store once when I noticed that my cart told the story of the wretched, lonely person I was—one can of tuna fish, soup, a small container of milk, cottage cheese, two avocados, a cantaloupe, and Frosted Flakes. I even remember my girlfriends inviting me to join them at a comedian's performance one night. I can't remember the guy's name, but his whole routine was about how men are Neanderthals. My girlfriends were laughing so hard they were crying. I was just crying.

So I started doing something physical to try to change my state of mind. I would sit in the car before I went in anywhere and look in the rearview mirror. I would smile the biggest, most clown-like smile I could muster. I would just sit there, sometimes shaking my head back and forth like a dog that won't let go of a toy. I would do this until I thought of something funny. I would do this until someone walked by and looked at me as if I were crazy, and that would feel funny. I would just do this until something genuinely funny came to my mind, and that was usually just how ridiculous I looked.

Humor is so healing. Laughing, the internal jogging, lightens us, unties the knots. One of the easy remedies for being stuck is to laugh—big, belly laughs if possible. Go rent a standup comedian on DVD or some funny movie. Go to a popular new Asian fusion restaurant and watch all of the tragically hip 21-year-olds talking on their cell phones while eating California rolls. Go to the zoo and watch the giraffes. Make yourself laugh. Don't bite the laugh off as it comes—let it out. Laugh until you break up your facade. Laugh so that little kids wonder what's wrong with you. And in that euphoric laughter, your body and spirit will begin to get unstuck.

You just can't stay tied up in painful knots when you're laughing. It's impossible. Laughter unties you whether you want it to or not. It reminds me of how sad I feel for some people who just can't laugh. You've seen them. The only ones in the room who sit stoically in the face of knee-slapping humor. I remember when I first started giving speeches to groups I would be so self-conscious about how I was being perceived. I would wonder, *Why isn't that woman in the front row laughing? That's the sternest face I've ever seen, and the rest of the room is cracking up. What's wrong with my presentation today?* After ten or so years of speaking regularly, I finally got it. People laugh when they want to laugh. Yes, they often need to be prompted with something funny, but some people can't let themselves go and laugh even in the midst of the most hysterical thing they've ever heard. And seeing their purposeful, determined faces is so sad. I want to bring them up on stage and ask them, "What makes you laugh? When do you laugh? How can I help you laugh today?" (Actually, I want to ask them if they've been giving flying lessons at a broom factory, but that's not very nice.) I know it's not about me. It's about them, and wherever they are, they're just not ready to get off that dead horse yet.

During that difficult time in my mid-30s, I started doing another physical motion that I still do today, which helps get me unstuck. It also looks funny, so I try not to do it in public, unless that's absolutely necessary. I started doing it in front of the big mirror in my bathroom, where I still do it sometimes. I'm not sure where the inspiration came from, but here it is. It's a little difficult to describe, more of a visual, but let me give it a try. I will swirl my right hand around at the wrist in a counterclockwise motion, and then release it into a wave. As I'm swirling, I'm thinking, *Bless,* and as I let go into the wave I think, *Release.* So it's bless . . . and release. There's another step too. As I say "Release" and start to wave, I lift my left foot up, so I'm a little off balance. Sometimes as I'm blessing and releasing, I'm thinking, *Go with God. BUT GO! And don't let the door hit you in the behind on your way out.*

It took me forty-two years, but I finally figured out that I can't fix anybody. I can't make my co-workers happy. I can't make my boss see what is praiseworthy. I can't make my kids appreciate me. If my colleagues are walking around resenting their jobs and complaining about everything, it's not my fault. I could bring bagels every day for a month, with specialty cream cheeses, and these sorrowful souls would still be miserable. Bless and release.

This is one of the many precious lessons I learned from my stepkids. And since the day I learned it, I've been able to apply it to every area of my life. Thank you, kids. What a gift you gave me without even realizing it. When I first came into their lives, they were as wary and suspicious of me as you can imagine. That was their job. They were being loyal to their mother, and they didn't believe they could love me and love their mother at the same time. I completely get it, and I got it then, but I thought I could wear them down. I thought, *If I just bake enough, if I just let them stay up late enough, if I just show enough interest in them as people—they will love me. I'm so loveable,* I thought. *What's not to love?*

I remember the suffering of those early years together. I remember their hard faces, so filled with pain, and my nervousness. I wanted so much to make them happy. I wanted to make them see how good their lives really were. I wanted them to see how much their father loved them, how he sacrificed to give them everything, how he would move heaven and earth to give them the world. I wanted them to see how they were warm and well-fed, how they had toys and friends and books, how they had grown-ups in their lives who truly loved them. I know their lives weren't perfect, that they wished their parents had stayed together, but I wanted them to see that there was so much to be grateful for. I wanted to make them feel something, something positive, have some hope for a brighter day. I wanted to earn their trust, maybe even their love someday. And I worked hard at it—for years—until the light bulb came on.

Whose business is it who they love?

Really. Is it any of my business who they love?

No. It's their business who they love. They may love me some-day. They may never love me. They may love their mom or their dad or neither. They may love each other or a spouse someday or good friends, or they may not. It's not my business. Bless and release.

I remember the day I got it. I didn't really talk about it with my husband or with them. I just got it. And that day I felt weight lifting off of my shoulders. I stopped hoping they'd hug me back when I hugged them. I hugged them when I wanted to and that was that. I cooked for them when I wanted to and didn't wait for the thank-you. I worked to save money for their college funds and took great pleasure in doing it. I focused on what I loved, instead of what they loved.

I love them. That's just the way it is. I love them, and I'm here for them whenever they need or want me. If their father died or went away tomorrow, I'd still love them. They're inside me now. And, by the way, I love their father. Loving him is just who I am. It's the best part of me. I love the son I gave birth to a year ago and the one I just gave birth to. I love all of our children. I love my job. I love the breeze coming through this window. And none of these loves depends on changing anyone else or waiting for anyone to do or feel anything.

I remember taking my one-year-old back to meet my parents a few months ago. It was a long trip, but so worth it, to see my par-ents watch Ethan's bright eyes looking everywhere. Ethan was hav-ing an attachment issue to his dad big-time during this trip. He wanted Aaron or no one, including me. He didn't want to let my mom hold him or my dad pick him up. He only wanted Aaron, and he screamed like the girls in horror movies if he didn't get him.

I know it made my mother feel funny that Ethan didn't cling to me. *If your son is going to cling to someone, shouldn't it be to you? Why is he so much more attached to his father than to you?* I would hold Ethan, rock him back and forth, and tell him everything was okay, but the screaming only stopped the second Aaron took him in his arms. And it stopped immediately when he did.

When I tell that story to my girlfriends, they're so supportive. "Oh, that must have made you feel terrible." But the truth is it didn't. The same lesson my stepkids taught me helped me so much in this situation. I love Ethan. And I know he loves me, but even if he doesn't—whose business is it who he loves? Whose business is it who he wants to hold him at this moment, who he wants to sit next to, who makes him feel safe and secure? It doesn't make me a bad parent if my son prefers his father right now or forever. It doesn't make me a bad parent if my stepkids don't tell me they love me. It doesn't make me a bad radio announcer if my show's ratings go down. I can control only what I can control—me and my heart.

Bless and release.

I trust now that everything is exactly as it should be—in all the work I do, in my relationships, in my body, in everything. This is not to say that I never have goals or never strive for anything. It is also not to say that bad things don't and won't happen, which I'm not expecting or wanting. It is only to say that I know that the life I am living today, with all of its apparent challenges, is exactly what I chose for myself. How do I know that I wanted to have three step-kids? Because I have them. That's how I know I wanted them. How do I know I wanted to be pregnant at forty-two? Because I am.

How do I know that I wanted to write this book? Because I'm writing it. I used to say that I wanted to write a book. Usually it was something I'd just say to myself, but I would occasionally share that thought with a close friend. I would get frustrated with myself as the years passed and I hadn't written a word, or the years would pass and I would write a paragraph here or there, a chapter here or there, but never on the same project. I would think, *If only I had more time, I could work on the book. If only I wasn't so busy all the time with my job, I could really spend time writing.*

That was a lie. It was a big fat lie that I was telling myself. The truth is I didn't want to write the book. If I had wanted to, I would have. Plain and simple. I know it now because the second I really wanted to write the book, I did. It's like people who say they want to lose weight, but never exercise. It's a lie that they want to lose weight. They don't really want to—and that may be perfectly okay—but what is definitely not okay is living with the stress of a personal lie that big.

How do you know you want what you have in your life right now? Because you have it. That's it. If you ever truly do want something else, then you'll have that. But until then, you'll have this. If you wanted a promotion in your job, you'd figure out a way to get it or you'd get another job where they valued your contribution more. If you wanted to make a million dollars, you would. There is money to be made out there. Just ask the YouTube guys. If you're not making the money you want to, it's because you don't really want to. You may have some truth hidden deep down inside you that says, "Money is the root of all evil," and you don't want to be evil—so you don't make money. Reread the scripture. It says *the love* of money is the root of all evil.

Even as I write these words, I know there is someone who will read them who will think, *I didn't choose for my husband to die,* or *I didn't choose for my child to have cancer.* I can hear your heart. Of course you didn't. I try to think about what I would feel if my husband were taken from me by some violent act or if my child were diagnosed with leukemia. How would I ever come to a place of moving forward? I don't know. I can't pretend to understand those emotions. I only know this—in my personal experience, every person who comes into my life blesses me somehow, and every person who leaves my life blesses me somehow. And every day, with whoever is present and whatever is happening, I believe there is beauty.

Bless and release.

CHAPTER NINE

Antidote to Criticism

"Brains, like hearts, go where they are appreciated."
—ROBERT S. MCNAMARA

There is an antidote to criticism, an anti-venom. It is one we can give ourselves and each other any time, and it's free. Plus, it's powerful. We've felt its power in our own lives, seen it change our co-workers and our children, experienced the pain of its absence. It is a motivator that can lead us toward our soul's work or steer us off course. It is potent enough to do either.

It is appreciation.

I heard the story once of a famous psychiatrist (or was it psychologist?) whose name I can't remember to save my life—but here's the important part. He was nearing the end of his life and his life's work. He had been laboring for years to complete the definitive treatise on what motivates man. What, of all the experiences or possessions, truly motivates a human being? Is it love? Hunger? Money? Power? Is it the search for eternal youth, the desire to change the world, the longing to procreate?

This doctor had a young assistant he had been dictating his book to, and one morning he called the assistant to him.

"I've just figured it out," the doctor said with light in his eyes. "I know now what it is that motivates mankind. We must begin again."

"But, Master, we are nearly finished with the work. You've written 800 pages, and you're almost there. How can we begin again?"

"Because we must. I've just figured out that what motivates man is appreciation. Let's start again with page one . . ."

Appreciation is the antidote to criticism. It may be the antidote to a number of other emotional maladies, such as frustration and resentment, but it is definitely the antidote to criticism, but perhaps not in the way you are thinking. Yes, it feels good to be appreciated. Better than good. It feels validating. We can do anything when we feel appreciated. We can create magnificent dinners every night when our husband and kids rave about our cooking. We can work weekends to hit sales goals when we feel the sincere pride and appreciation of our sales manager. We can stay up all night helping our kids with a project if we feel the warmth and relief in their bodies when they throw their arms around our necks to thank us.

Yes, appreciation is a motivator. When we receive it, it can motivate us to do amazing things. But if we want to come out of the funk of criticism, receiving it may not work.

No, we must *give* it. It's like the beautiful girl who is convinced she's ugly who cannot hear your compliments. It's the talented young man who is doing so well in school, but who rolls his eyes when you tell him how proud you are of him. These precious young people are in a place so dark, hopefully just stumbling around in the fog of teenage hormones, that they can't receive your appreciation, can't take your praise to their hearts.

You and I are in the same distant place when we are stung by criticism. If our supervisor makes a joke at our expense in front of our peers, then laughs and says, "Just kidding," we are hurt. As we leave the meeting, one of our co-workers (who maybe should be the supervisor) pulls us aside: "Hey, Jim. I just want you to know how much we all appreciate the job you do around here. You take our calls all day long, never complain about our endless questions, help all of us be better. Thank you." That kind of camaraderie and encouragement can pull us out of the pain caused by criticism, but it doesn't always work. Sometimes we just can't hear it. "Thanks," we mutter as we walk away to do some serious stewing about our boss's comments.

Here is what I'm sure *will* work, every time. Think of it as taking a pill you need to restore your heartbeat, your life. You've been bitten by a snake. The snake may be your boss or your spouse or your teenager, even your mother. That snake may not have intended to bite you, but he did and you're withering. You need medicine—fast. Don't wait. Search your mind immediately for the first thing you feel grateful for. It can be anything or anyone. If you're at 7-Eleven, and the guy behind the counter tells you your taillight is out, maybe saving you from getting pulled over coming home some night later that week, you thank him. You sincerely thank him and tell him how kind that was. You take a minute to e-mail your 13-year-old's teacher and thank her for showing genuine interest in your daughter. You tell her that her class is the only one your daughter ever talks about, that she comes to life when she's studying this subject, and how much you appreciate her. The next time you see the assistant on the fourth floor who is always so welcoming and helpful, you tell her: "Can I just tell you how much I appreciate you? So many people are so stressed out and negative around this place, but every time you walk into the room, it lightens. You follow through and you're courteous, even when people are demanding. You're just awesome."

Now, if you're feeling like Gandhi and really getting good at this antidote thing, you could send the appreciation right back at the person who hurt you. Sometimes you may not be able to think of something you appreciate about your boss, at least not at that moment. "I appreciate that you sign my checks every week. Uh, wait a minute, you don't sign my checks. Well, never mind." Or maybe the critic is your wife. You go back to the bedroom to change clothes, and you're steaming from sharp words she just spoke to you. But remember, you're getting good at this, and you know showing appreciation to her will heal you and may even heal her. So you think about something you love about her, something you are grateful for, and when your face has calmed down (don't wait too long), you walk back into the kitchen and tell her, "Honey, I appreciate you so much. I appreciate that you keep our kids alive all day. I'm around them for five minutes and they nearly kill themselves at least once, sticking their fingers in sockets and doing headers off the couch. You do a great job with them. And I want you to know that I see it." Don't wait around for the hug or the thanks; it may not come right away. Your work is done there. Go downstairs now.

Okay. Time for Life Advanced, a 500-level class. This next piece is for black diamond skiers. You're ready to hit from the black tees now. You're playing the tips. You've been showing appreciation for others, not only as an antidote to criticism, but more regularly in your life. You've been feeling its power and gaining respect for it as a force of nature and not just some sappy sentiment. Now comes the biggest challenge of all (at least for me). Does it work when the perpetrator and the victim are both you? What is the antidote to your own endless self-criticism?

You may not even think of it as self-criticism. It has been so deeply ingrained in you for so long, you don't see it. It likely started in your youth when an adult you trusted said something negative to you about yourself, and you believed him—and somewhere deep down inside you still do. Your mother may have told you that you were too big for ballet, or maybe she said, "We just don't have artistic talent in this family." Or maybe your father said that you shouldn't feel badly about not having athletic ability, he never did, either. It just isn't in your genes. Or a trusted aunt or uncle said that you shouldn't worry about saving for college because the best you could do was marry a rich man anyway. Or your older brother told you that everybody who has money must have done something unethical to get it. "Nobody gets rich putting in a hard day's work," he said, and you believed him.

Who knows who it came from, and frankly, who cares? That person likely didn't intend to scar you for life. He didn't wake up that morning and wonder what he could say to you that would limit your potential and make you doubt yourself well into your 60s. You can't go back and fix that person or that moment. Now, that person may still be in your life, still saying little hurtful, degrading things, or that person may be gone now. Even if she has passed away, the criticism continues because now you're saying it to yourself. You don't need her to tell you you're fat. You do it ten times a day for her.

Let's look at some of the beliefs that might be keeping you from having joy in your work and in your life. You may believe that you're not bright enough to ever make it to the top. You may think that you aren't smart enough to get into college or stick it out once you're there (let alone enjoy it). You may think that you're not talented enough to make it in movies or music or art or literature. Those are fields for people who are "talented." You may think that your job is all you're capable of doing, and you may be passing these self-doubts on to your children without realizing it. Remember—example, example, example.

Are you ever late for work because you just can't find anything to wear that you don't look hideous in? Are you ever late to work because you're just too down on your life to get in the shower? Do you ever tell your child, "Maybe we can go to the park later, sweetheart" because you just don't want to see the other mothers? Do you spend any of your day in resentment, whether it's of your co-worker who got the job or the raise you wanted or your children who get to sleep in and eat whatever they want without gaining weight? If so, self-criticism could be at play here, sometimes expressed through a passive-aggressive mean-spiritedness toward others and sometimes through a dagger you throw yourself on.

What works on this limiting belief system? How can I expect to help you with put-downs you've been reminding yourself of for so many decades that they're embedded in your psyche? Well, it's because I know what works and it's easy. I don't know why nobody ever told me this, but it's so easy you may doubt that it's real. You may over-think it and believe that moving forward requires $50,000 worth of therapy or losing fifty pounds. Nothing wrong with either of those things, but they're not necessary to begin having joy in your work and in your life. You can do that right now before you even put this book down.

Appreciate. Do it silently right now. Appreciate your paycheck, if you have one. If you don't, appreciate the source of your money, whatever it is. If it's your spouse, appreciate him. If it's your ex-spouse, appreciate him too (c'mon—you can do it). If it's your inheritance or your royalties or your church's or the government's welfare system, appreciate it. Feel it in your heart. "Oh, thank you. Thank you for helping me. Thank you for this food I eat, these clothes my children wear, this chance for another day." Feel it, and as you do, feel your heart expand.

I have always believed that once the heart expands, it never goes back to its original size. It's the Grinch principle. Remember in *How the Grinch Stole Christmas!* how the Grinch's heart starts to grow as he shows love and receives love? Maybe that is why appreciation is so powerful. When you appreciate, your heart expands. It now has more room, more room to fill with love for your family, more room to fill with patience for your boss, more room for new ideas you can nurture and develop. And remember—whatever you practice, you get good at. If you're practicing blaming your parents for everything that's wrong with you or practicing blaming your ex for everything that's wrong with your life, that is the only skill you'll develop. Blame. You could win the gold medal for blame, but it's not an Olympic sport. It's not any sport or other worthwhile activity. It is an insult to your Maker because it wastes the precious gift of life you were given. It is a crippling habit that you can replace with a new habit called appreciation. Blame is probably harder to give up than smoking, the payoff is so huge, but you can do it if you long to find out what the good life really feels like.

I have tried, really put effort into trying to control my thoughts. I've tried to do this on various subjects. I know there are many people—writers, philosophers, and clergymen—who believe that it's possible to accomplish this. They may be right, but I owe you my truth here—I've never been able to do it. I don't know if it's possible or not for other people. You may be able to control your own thoughts. If so, e-mail me and share with me how you do it. But for me, if I tell myself to stop thinking about where I'm going to come up with the money for the kids' Christmas, what's the first thing I think of? Right—how to come up with the money for the kids' Christmas. If I tell myself to stop obsessing about the snotty woman at work who said something critical about me to a friend, who then repeated it to me, do you think my brain obeys? Of course not. I just obsess more.

I just don't know how to make my brain stop thinking a thought. I can't stop thinking about a double cheeseburger even when I know I should. I can't stop thinking about something irritating or annoying or negative even though I know it's not good for me. Thoughts just appear in my brain, like rain clouds. They come, and they go, and sometimes they come back again. But they do not bend to my will.

So I squeeze them out. I get so interested and engaged in other things that there is no room, or at least very little room, for them. I love living my life so much that I don't have time to wish my life had turned out differently. I love loving my kids so much that I don't have time to wish they were different or that I had more of them or fewer. I love my husband so much that I don't have time to look for what I'd like to change about him. There just isn't time for appreciating him and resenting him in the same marriage.

Can I make myself stop thinking self-degrading thoughts? No. Occasionally I pass a mirror and still obsess about the size of my behind. From time to time I find myself wishing I was petite or more feminine. I wish my nose was smaller, or my waist, or my feet. Sometimes I wish I had been more ambitious, gone after bigger jobs when I was younger, made more money. But these thoughts don't last for long, and they almost make me laugh right now because there just isn't room in my life for them. Sorry. Go with God, but GO!!

Appreciation is a way of life for me now, and it's not a habit that I apply to everyone else but me. I appreciate myself, too. I appreciate that I know how to laugh, loudly and often. I appreciate that I love to work and can do many different things to earn money for my family. I appreciate that I can forgive, quickly if not easily, and free my heart from that pain. I appreciate that I am a good mom to my kids—not perfect, not always as loving and patient as I'd like, but good. I appreciate my beauty, my brain, my family, my parents, my Creator. I appreciate this precious life—so much that I don't make room for dying every day. Death will come soon enough. While I'm alive, I want to live.

My dear sister Connie, who is an amazingly kind and wise woman and mother, used to talk about the "devil on your shoulder." It's been so many years since she's told me this story that I hope I'm remembering it correctly, but it went something like this.

When you want to do something you know you shouldn't, that's the devil on your shoulder. You just shoo him right off and let the good angel on your other shoulder help you do the right thing.

That image of the devil on my shoulder stuck with me, and now I see it like this. The devil on my shoulder is a grudge. To hold a grudge is to invite the devil to plop down right on your shoulder and weigh you down every day. To hold resentment or blame for anything or anyone in your life—including yourself—is to pull out the La-Z-Boy right on your shoulder and invite the devil to have a seat.

Shoo that devil off of there. You can't take care of yourself or your family with a devil sitting on your shoulder. How do you expect to succeed in your job, really thrive and grow, when you're distracted all day by a grudge you're holding against your boss or your colleague? How do you think you can love and care for your children when you're weighted down with resentment for their father?

How can you function at all, accomplish the smallest tasks, hear the angels sing, when there is a devil on your shoulder?

Get him off of there. Shoo, fly. Shoo! I know you can do it. Remember—it's not hard, it's just different. It's a new skill. Let go of the grudge through appreciation. Fill your heart with gratitude and laughter, and you won't even notice the devil disappearing. One day you'll just feel lighter. You'll wonder why getting up for work feels easier. You'll smile when you realize you can't remember the last time you spoke in anger, and the devil will be gone.

Just like that.

CHAPTER TEN

Faith Moves

*"I'm a great believer in luck, and I find the harder I work the more
I have of it."*

—THOMAS JEFFERSON

It's scary to jump into your own life, just like it's scary to jump into
the deep end of a pool from the high dive. You're not sure what it
will feel like the first time you do it. It may sting. The water may be
cold. You may get water up your nose. It's easier to sit on the side-
lines and watch other people try it. Some of them flop. Some make
a huge splash. You can watch them without commitment. You can
make fun of them from the safety of your towel on the grass nearby.
You can tell yourself you're safe there, that you're just waiting, that
maybe you'll try it later. From that position you can criticize those
who do jump in, heckle them, tease them as they emerge from the
water. Or maybe you can study how they do it, compare techniques,
consider how you might do it if you ever decide to jump in.

But faith does not wait. Faith moves. Faith applies for the job,
proposes marriage, says yes to the new assignment, sings out loud.
Faith takes a child into foster care, volunteers to be a Big Brother
or Big Sister, takes tap dancing lessons—at 50—and falls in love at

any age. Faith sees the sunrise and not the yard that needs more landscaping. Faith sees the child's smile and not the applesauce all over his face. Faith doesn't resent the commute but feels grateful to have a job and a car to get there in.

Faith may study and learn, but at some point faith realizes she has researched enough. Faith moves. I think I've spent most of my adult life studying how to write a novel. I may or may not have learned something from all of those books on how to write fiction, how to write dialogue and develop character, how to keep your reader going from chapter to chapter. Years ago, I had the thrill of meeting novelist Dan Brown, author of *The Da Vinci Code* and several other best-sellers. He visited my hometown as part of a gathering for alumni of Phillips Exeter Academy, a prep school in New Hampshire we both had the honor of attending (from which he actually graduated). Anyway, my husband and I had the chance to take Dan and his wife on a tour of the city and have a little lunch. (As I recall, Dan even bought.)

Aaron and I were like kids in a candy store, asking too many questions, so thrilled to be able to just sit and visit with two fascinating minds such as Dan and Blythe Brown. We told them about our closet desires to write a novel, and they listened patiently, even offered feedback and suggestions. Dan recommended we read a small paperback book entitled *How to Write a Blockbuster*. We both did. I think I read it three times. I may have learned something from it. What I did not learn from it or any of the other books I read was how to begin. That is not something I can learn. That is something I must simply do.

I think the key is this. You've got to do things before you are sure you'll be good at them. You've got to risk stinking. This is the beginner's mind, the beginner's spirit. And while the occasional first-timer has beginner's luck and dazzles people with his first attempt, most of us flop our first time out. We play lousy golf our first time off the tee. We pray just to make contact with the ball so we don't completely humiliate ourselves. We sing off key the first time we try out for the choir. We are awkward the first time we ask a girl for a date. We get shown the door the first time we ask for a raise.

So what? I think we place too much emphasis on not failing. We give lip service to failure being an important part of learning, but we all do everything imaginable to keep it from ever happening to us and recoil in horror if it does. We are terrified of the flop. And I'm not saying we have to rejoice when it happens. We should always do our best, but the fear of failure is just too paralyzing. We need to experience it more often so we can get good at it, or at least get comfortable with the jumping-in process (which can, and often does, lead to failure).

This concept feels strange to embrace. "Embrace failure? What, are you nuts? You want to get good at failing?" No. I want to get good at doing, and if you do enough you will fail. The only way to protect yourself from failure is to sit beside the pool and not jump in. How boring! That's not why you were born. You were born to live, to engage, to attempt, to fail AND to succeed—all of it.

I heard a woman speak once who described it like this—it's sort of like the saying from when we were kids: "It's one for the money. Two for the show. Three to get ready. And four to go." (Actually, that makes me think of Elvis.) But here's how most of us live. "It's one for the money. Two for the show. Three to get ready . . . Three to get ready . . . Three to geeeettttttt readddddyyyyyyyy. Hold on, I'll do it when I lose twenty pounds. I'll do it when the kids are grown up. I'll do it after the mortgage is paid off and the kids are through college and . . ." We never do it. We die in "three to get ready."

That is my biggest fear. I fear that one day, heaven forbid, I'll be killed in some sudden and tragic accident, and I'll have that moment before breath leaves me when I know it's over. In that moment, I'll think of my dear husband and my precious children, and then I'll think, *Oh, Amanda, you could have been . . . Reba McEntire. But no. You died with your music in you.* We spend our whole lives tuning our instruments, and we never play. Why? Because we're afraid we won't be good enough. We're afraid someone will tell us we stink, or even worse, we're afraid they won't listen at all.

So let's go there. If having someone tell us we stink is the worst thing that can happen to us for trying something new, will that kill us? What if you paint or sculpt and actually get a show, and nobody comes? Will that kill you? What if they come and nobody buys anything? Will that kill you? What if you sacrifice all your time and money and effort to go to law school and then lose your first big case? Will that kill you? What if the big firm you've always wanted to work for doesn't hire you in the first place? That won't kill you, will it?

As I've said, I've had eighteen jobs in my forty-two years, and I've been good at only a handful of them. Truly. At most of them I was mediocre at best, and at some I flat-out stunk. I may have excelled at one or two, but not the majority—that's for sure. I remember my first job. Don't we all remember our first job? It's like remembering our first love. (What was his name?) I don't often tell this story because I'm afraid of sending the wrong message to young people, but I lied about my age to get a job one summer at an Orange Julius in the University Mall near Brigham Young University. I think I was thirteen at the time, and I told the manager I was sixteen. I could have passed for twenty, so I don't blame him at all. The only real stickler came the day he handed me his car keys and told me to run down to the local grocery to get some lettuce and such for the restaurant. Yikes! I couldn't tell him I didn't know how to drive because I was three years under the legal age, so I took the keys, then ran like the wind all the way to the store. I got the lettuce and tomatoes and whatever else he had asked for and ran all the way back. As I walked into the store, sweating like I had just done the Ironman triathlon, he asked, "What took you so long?"

It might have been that incident, or maybe the paperwork on my Social Security number came back, but he eventually figured out I was his youngest employee by a few years and fired me. Sigh. I guess that was a failure, but what a thrill to work there at all. I'm not proud of having lied or of having been fired, but I am proud of having worked. I remember learning the recipes for strawberry-banana and peach Juliuses. I remember rotating hot dogs and hanging hot pretzels from hooks. I remember keeping my two uniform tops clean and handling it when twenty people walked up all at the same time and I had to move fast. I remember opening up the metal gates in the morning if I worked the first shift. And I remember coming around the counter and wiping tables when things would slow down, kibitzing with the people who worked in neighboring stores. I loved that job. If my old boss is reading this, I'm sorry I lied.

I remember the first job when I told the truth about my age. It was at a little restaurant called Kemler's on Route 11 in Bloomsburg, Pennsylvania. The restaurant was just down the hill from my house. I loved the way it smelled. I loved the couples and truckers and families who came in regularly. I wanted every shift the Kemlers would give me. The husband and wife who owned the restaurant were such good people: kind and patient and loving, just like parents to me. I learned how to keep coffee cups full, recommend pie, and carry three plates of open-faced roast beef sandwiches with mashed potatoes and gravy on one arm. At the time, I thought that was the greatest feat of my young life, and I still think it's up there in my top five skills.

Now let me tell you about the time I tried to get a slice of lemon meringue out of the pie tin and onto a plate. First one I blew. It got all goopy and looked like pudding. Second one, same. Third one I cut bigger, thinking size was my problem, but the meringue fell off just the same. I was down to one slice left, and I took it out and served it in the tin. Got the best tip of the night. I don't even remember how much coffee I spilled on people in that restaurant. I do remember bumping ketchup bottles at the end of my shift. ("Bumping" bottles is taking what's left in one and using it to fill up another so every table has a full bottle.) I bumped a little too hard on one and broke the glass, sending shard-laden ketchup all over the table. Mrs. Kemler just smiled and handed me a wet rag.

Ketchup happens.

Faith doesn't wait. Faith moves. I once took a job as a reception-ist at a hair salon called Hairport. (Isn't that cute?—Hairport.) It was located in the basement of a building that had a chiropractor's office on the first floor. I sat at the desk and answered the phones. I would book appointments for perms and cuts and shampoo/sets. And then one day, one of the stylists got so far behind in her sched-ule (actually—that happened quite frequently) that she asked me to shampoo her next client so she would be ready. I had never shampooed anyone before. But, hey—I had *been* shampooed. How hard could it be?

I went to the waiting area and got the older woman and escorted her back to the sink. I remembered to put the plastic cape on (good), and then eased her back until her neck was resting on the towel on the edge of the basin. I turned on the hose and proceeded to send scalding hot water down her ear canal at fifty miles an hour. I don't remember if she screamed. The sound may have been coming from me. But I remember apologizing as if my life depended on it. I'd never been so sorry for anything before. I had hurt someone— someone's mother. That dear woman actually let me try again. Can you imagine? I checked the temperature this time and barely let the water trickle over her head. I'm sure she still had lots of conditioner in her hair when she finally got to the stylist, but at least I hadn't damaged her inner ear any more than I already had.

Just thinking about that moment gives me the shivers now. How embarrassing! Not as embarrassing as the time I was a waitress and came out of the bathroom with three feet of toilet paper stuck to the heel of my shoe, but still pretty embarrassing. Was it a failure? (The hair washing, not the toilet paper.) It sure wasn't a success, but what I am proud of is that when that sweet woman told me to try again, I overcame my fear and did just what she asked.

The things we get to do, the work we get to accomplish, when we're not afraid of being a beginner! I have had two stints in management. This may be something many of you want to experience in your careers, or perhaps you're already the head of a team and handling the challenges with creativity and persistence. Either way, I am familiar enough with the challenge of managing to know that most managers feel like a complete failure at least once a week. A key employee quits. Numbers don't add up. You go over your budget or lose an important client. This stuff happens to every manager every month. So what? The key is what happens right after the fall.

I offer this opinion humbly because I must tell you, of my two experiences, which were twenty years apart, my first was more successful than not, and my second was a total failure. Which one do you think I learned more from?

My first experience was working as the shift manager at a steak house. I scheduled employees, trained new employees, stepped in wherever I was needed in a shift. I loved working with those people. Most of them were teenagers, just a few years younger than me at the time. I loved showing them that I would wash dishes with them, refill the salad bar, run the register—whatever they needed. I earned their respect, and they worked crazy hours for me as a result. I remember New Year's Eves in the restaurant. We'd close at 11:00 P.M. and try so hard to get out before midnight, but we'd never make it. At twelve o'clock, I'd turn on the intercom and shout, "Happy New Year!" And I loved hearing all their voices echoing back from the walk-ins and fryers and dining room, "Happy New Year!"

Back then, I ate a Number 5 (nice cut of sirloin with a baked potato and Texas toast) five or six nights a week for a couple of years. Man, can you imagine eating that much meat? I can't now, but back then it was salad bar for breakfast and Number 5 for dinner. I learned so much from being trusted with that team of employees. I learned from watching how my behavior and attitude affected them, and I learned from just trying. I learned how to order food for the restaurant because the owner trusted me to do it. I ordered way too much the first time, and we had garbanzo beans coming out our ears for a few months. But I learned. I learned what a good team felt like when it was humming along. Nothing like a Saturday night, with a line out the door and the sound of waitresses laughing with customers in the dining room.

Fast forward twenty years to when the management of my radio station trusted me with the role of program director for a brand new station they had just purchased. Actually, they'd purchased the right to broadcast on a frequency. Everything else we built from scratch. Our engineers built the towers from scratch. We commissioned new jingles, hired new salespeople and an entire staff of new announcers. The station was unique in two respects. First, it was a talk format targeting women, a format that, as far as we knew, was then only being implemented on three other stations in the country. So we were breaking new ground. And second, with one or two exceptions, every talk-show host we hired had never done the job before.

What were we thinking? We were thinking that we didn't want announcers or people who sounded like announcers. We wanted real people—people women could relate to and possibly come to trust, people who cared about politics and the terrible two's and everything in between. I remember approaching people I respected, people I liked, and asking them if they would ever consider doing a radio show. "What, are you nuts?" was a common response, but then they'd think it over, and sometimes they'd come around.

I loved that station. *Love* is not too strong a word. I loved it. I loved the way it sounded, the people who worked on the air and off, what it stood for. I loved going out with the salespeople to talk potential sponsors into taking a leap of faith with us. I loved meeting with the on-air hosts every week, feeling their energy, hearing their passion for this new infant of a station. I even loved going to management meetings and planning for the future.

As it turned out, there wasn't much of a future. The station was on the air just over a year. It never showed up in the Arbitron ratings, the bible for radio stations all over the country, so ownership and upper management pulled the plug. I don't blame them at all. It was their money going out the door every month, and there was nothing to convince them that the future would be any brighter than the present. I don't blame the employees either. They were fantastic and getting better all the time. I blame me. When you have big talent on a team and a losing record, you fire the coach. I wish they had fired me sooner and seen if a more talented leader could have guided the station in a way that would have kept it alive.

Oh, I hate being fired, even when it happens as nicely as it did this last time. Being fired is like going through a divorce—in its most amicable form, it still hurts like the dickens. When the station was taken off the air, my GM told me repeatedly that I had talent as a manager and that I would be in management again someday in some capacity if I wanted to be. She was kind. I'm not sure she was accurate.

Don't get me wrong. I'm not afraid to try it again. If a similar opportunity came along and the feeling was right, I'm sure I'd jump in again. That's who I am. But I am also starting to learn enough about myself to understand that I am a better player than a coach. I like to work out, run drills, put on the uniform, have the spotlight on me. I don't thrive on power. I thrive on playing. I want to be in the game.

This may have been why I was such a lousy lawyer.

If you are currently in a job that you spent years preparing to do, took out student loans to pay for the education, maybe even planned to follow in your father's footsteps, I know that place. My hope is that the work you spent your life thinking you were meant to do *is* in fact fulfilling for you. If it's not, if you feel as though you're living someone else's life, but the thought of leaving the store, the farm, the profession sends you into utter panic, listen up. This story is for you.

My father is a lawyer, a fine and trusted counselor to many. I grew up hearing him tell stories about his cases, about judges and arguments and briefs. I loved the stories. I love my father, and I always wanted to be like him. So when I neared the end of college and couldn't think of anything better to do, I applied to go to law school. As I recall now, I think it took me two years to get in. The first year I was rejected, so I went back and took more college classes and gave it another shot.

I went to law school for nearly two years before I dropped out. That should have been a clue to me that I didn't want to be a lawyer, but seven years later, after the stigma of being a dropout had nagged me into near insanity, I applied to reenter law school and was granted the privilege. The second time around, I actually enjoyed it. I was older, more confident, had enough perspective to not let silly things intimidate me. Things like a professor asking a question I didn't know the answer to. That used to make me itch with humiliation. Being a little older and more experienced, I wasn't as obsessed with trying to impress these professors in their tweed jackets and Hush Puppies shoes. I was paying them to teach me— they should worry about impressing me! I also realized that the diploma hanging on my wall is just as pretty as the one earned by the student who made herself insane trying to get all A's. (I may be just a little jealous here.) Not getting A's did not reduce the joy I had in the experience. In fact, it may have increased it because it took my life off the burner. I learned under some pressure, surely, but not under a false pressure I put on myself.

When I finally graduated, I was amazed to be offered a job at one of the top law firms in the state. This was a firm with heritage. One of its founders practically wrote the code in many areas of state law. The managing partner was a well-respected litigator and criminal defense attorney who knew everyone and was not to be trifled with. And he wanted me? I think that may be a decision he's reconsidered since then.

I was a workhorse for the firm. That is for sure. I think I worked every weekend for at least the first year. I read endless cases, researched countless briefs, made some good arguments along the way—but in general, was a complete flop. I remember getting so upset during a negotiation that I broke out in hives all along my jaw line. I nearly broke out in tears I was so hurt on behalf of my clients. I remember getting my hide chewed by a judge once because I had assumed that one state's law applied, and he suggested (with some irritation) that I should have considered that Nevada law might apply. After my face and chest went totally red, my boss (who was letting me have a learning experience) got up and came to my defense. He had to come to my defense in front of a judge!! I was miserable. Nobody missed me when I left, except maybe my boss—who liked my laugh a lot more than he liked my work. (I miss him, too, come to think of it.)

I am more proud of the day I gave my month's notice to the law firm than I am proud of most things in my life. I am proud of it because the thought of leaving the practice after I had sacrificed so much to get there was terrifying, and I did it anyway. I am proud of it because it was one of the first times in my life when I stood up for my soul. "This is not who I am," I announced to myself and the world. I remember being as afraid to tell my father as I was to tell my boss. I didn't want my father to be disappointed. We fathers' daughters are like that. His response made me gasp. "Oh, Amanda. If I had the kind of talent you have, I probably wouldn't have been a lawyer, either." What? Was he kidding? I thought for so many years that he wanted me to be a lawyer when all along he only wanted me to be happy. Oh, fathers—be clear with your daughters—we can get confused so easily where our heroes are concerned.

To any of my former clients who are reading this book, I'm sorry. I'm sorry I wasn't the strong advocate you needed. Forgive me. And to the rest of you . . . see? It didn't kill me to stink, even at the job I had prepared most of my life to do. It didn't kill me to be humiliated in front of other lawyers or clients or even judges. It didn't kill me to leave it all behind after ten years of work.

Jump in, comrades. The water's fine.

CHAPTER ELEVEN

Your Best Is Good Enough

"Getting fired is nature's way of telling you that you had the wrong job in the first place."

—EDGAR BERGEN

O ne of the wonderful things about being fired is that it tells you something crucial about yourself, gives you information you may not be able to get in any other way. Sometimes it tells you this job isn't you, at least this incarnation of the job isn't you. Many, maybe most, people who are fired know it's coming—or should know. If every day is a struggle, if the joy has long since gone out of your work, if you stare off into space at your cubicle, if you dread the sound of your CEO's voice on your voice mail, you're already fired—it's just that no one has yet had the courage to act on the obvious.

It's almost like the person who has to get sick in order to take some time off. She's just not in tune enough with her body, not secure enough in who she is, to give herself the gift of rest and downtime, so when she needs it, her body gets the flu. Does that sound familiar? Getting fired is sometimes the same thing. Most people who get fired know the job isn't right for them. They know.

They may have secretly (or not so secretly) been wishing they had a different job for years but lacked the courage and confidence to go for it. So the universe steps in for them and gives them what they need. They get fired.

I've had several friends at work who have been fired and for whom that has been a huge gift. I remember watching them struggle, so out of sorts every day, never happy. If they got a bonus, it wasn't a big enough bonus. If they got called in to work, the manager should have bothered someone else. If they didn't get called in, the manager must be overlooking their talents. It was painful to care for them and watch them be so miserable. And the thing was—what they complained about might have been true—but it didn't matter. They could never change their manager's behavior. They could only affect the way they felt, and they felt lousy—all the time.

I remember the days these individuals were fired. Each of the ones I'm thinking of now was hurt, wounded by the dismissal. They stewed for varying lengths of time afterward. But with one exception, I think each of them is happier now. They just weren't in the right place for their spirit. Either it was the wrong kind of work or the wrong place to work. Maybe it just wasn't a good fit. But whatever it was, they were cramped and stuck and needed to get out. They needed to quit, but for reasons they must have perceived as important at the time, they couldn't. So they were fired. And then they were free.

Sometimes people get fired for a different but also life-affirming reason. They get fired because they stretched beyond what they knew they could do for sure. If you've been fired for this reason, you should be proud of it.

You wanted to run the department, so you went for it. You got the assignment, but you stunk. Everything became chaotic. Key players started threatening to leave. You got no respect in your meetings. And eventually you got fired. Bravo! You went for it. You extended yourself.

Or maybe you auditioned for a play. You were cast in a key role. But the first couple of performances you were so stiff, the director had to can you. Bravo again. You went for it.

I was fired from one of my favorite jobs. (Actually, I think my editor used the word *downsized.*) I had wanted to write a column for the *Salt Lake Tribune* for years. I started at a much smaller local paper called *The Event Newspaper.* It was, as I recall, a twice-monthly free publication with some pretty uneventful stuff in it—most uneventful of all being my column. I was proud of having gotten the column in the first place. I remember going to the paper with two sample columns in hand. They were garbage, really. They were little gossipy snippets I'd pulled off the wire at the radio station where I was working at the time. You could have seen the same stuff on any episode of *Entertainment Tonight.* What was I thinking? Well, I was thinking I'd put my own local and hopefully humorous spin on it, and I was thinking I'd help them fill space in the paper, and I was cheap. (It was that last thing that worked for me.)

A part of me was so shocked when I got that job. They were seriously going to let me write a column with my picture and name on the top. Wow! I'd better think of something to say. And I did, barely. I think I was paid $25 per column, far more than it was worth, but I learned about deadlines and observing life with the writer's eye and about finding something to say. I learned enough that after a year or so, I thought I was ready to try something a little more challenging, so I applied to a larger weekly paper called *The Private Eye.* This was a tabloid-sized paper, free in newsstands and nightclubs, that ran some original stories, several columns, and boatloads of personal ads. It was antiestablishment in its orientation and quite political. I pitched a weekly column in which I would feature people and events. The editor, who was also the publisher, accepted my proposal. He paid me $50 a column—I had doubled my salary. And now I was going to tackle some serious subjects.

I wrote that column for just about a year and struggled every week. I would write a column, then pick up the new issue to check it out and find myself reading a piece with my name at the bottom that I hadn't written. The editor, both the original one and the one he hired later as the paper grew, didn't like my work. They wanted an angry young woman who would write about being dissatisfied with government and politicians and people in general. They didn't want funny observations about life. They wanted Ann Coulter, or probably a liberal version of Ann.

I finally went to the publisher as the year ended and said, "You're not happy with my work, are you?" "No," he replied with no sugar coating. I appreciated his honesty. I thanked him for the chance he had given me, left the funky little office, which was located between a bar and a tattoo parlor, and got a job at the *Salt Lake Tribune* the next week.

Oh, baby! I was in the big time now. (Okay—if you're reading this in any major city that has a fabulous newspaper, you may be cracking up right now.) But for me, it was the big time. When the editor of the *Tribune* agreed to meet with me, I nearly fell over. I had wanted to meet him for so long, and now was my chance. As we walked into the restaurant for lunch that day, I was all ready to pitch him on a lifestyle column, maybe something for the Wednesday or Saturday edition, hopefully humorous. Before I could open my mouth, he said in his characteristic gruff voice, "Amanda. I want you to write a sports column."

That is when I laughed too loudly for a public place.

"What? Are you nuts?" I whispered back loudly, trying to recover. "I don't even know what clipping is. I mean, I grew up a Penn State fan, but only one of those fans who knows what Joe Paterno looks like, not one who knows who they're recruiting this year. I can't do this!"

"I know you *can*," he replied while sipping soup. "And I don't want a stat guy. I have lots of those. I want a female fan. I need to attract female readers to the sports page, and they won't come for stats, but they might come for you."

Long pause.

"Will you do it?" he pushed. We hadn't even had our entrée yet. I thought he'd wait until later in the meal to get down to it. If I said no, what would we talk about during lunch, or would we have to get our food to go?

"Yes!" I replied triumphantly.

"Good," he said with food in his mouth. "All you have to do is observe a sporting event each week and then write your column about your experience. Piece of cake."

I must admit. I liked the sound of that. No more angry young woman.

Oh, I loved being a sports columnist. My dad loved my being a sports columnist. I don't think I had ever felt so cool as when I wrote that column, even though the other sports writers treated me like I had leprosy. I knew they didn't think I knew what I was doing and didn't think I should be contaminating their sports pages with mindless drivel. They were probably right, on both counts. But, oh—how I loved it!

I'd go to basketball games and baseball games, gymnastic meets and the finish lines of marathons. I'd write about particular players whose facial expressions told me something, or sometimes I'd write about the wait in the hot dog line or maybe about some misbehaving fans. I remember one Utah Jazz game. It was a boring game as I recall. I think we were playing the Timberwolves. (That would probably be a great game now, but not back then, during the Stockton-to-Malone days. Back then we could beat everybody except Michael Jordan.) Anyway, there was a couple seated about ten rows in front of us, slightly off to the left, and they were having a big ole hairy fight. We (and by "we" I mean everybody in my section of the Delta Center) did not mean to eavesdrop, but we couldn't help it. They were loud! And they were so attractive it was hard to take your eyes off them. Everyone kept looking at everyone else with that expression that says, "They're not with me," and pretended to watch the game.

When I got home that night, I wrote my column about them. Now, you should know, I didn't put their names in the paper. I didn't know their names. But the woman later called me. She said, "How dare you put my personal private business in the *Salt Lake Tribune?!*" If I had been a mom at the time, I would have put her in time-out. As it was, I thought about it for a moment, still stunned that she had called me at all, and replied, "How dare you air your dirty laundry in front of 20,000 people? What were you thinking? You should have been on the JumboTron."

I don't know if that was the trigger, or the fact that the sports editor would rather be on *Fear Factor* eating maggots than read one more of my columns, or what, but I was let go. *Downsized,* was the official word. My poor sportswriter heart was broken, and I hadn't even had a chance to get a trench coat or put on weight yet. My life as a sports guy (gal) was over. I would never get to sit at the special table, make unsupported predictions about the outcome of games, eat the bad complimentary food, or feel as though I had a reason to be watching somebody else's kids play soccer. I was so dejected. My coolness had left the building.

But I had stretched! I am proud of being fired from that job. And I know I'll write another column someday, if I'm meant to. Saying yes to that column was saying yes to life, to passion and joy and my endless potential. (I know. That sounds like one of those affirmation cards.) When I got fired, after I got over the initial sadness of not being good enough, I realized all that the job had given me. It told me I could do anything, perhaps anything other than be an astronaut. If a woman who knew nothing about sports could write a sports column, what else could I do that I had never considered before? It was thrilling and eye-opening. It even led to my getting two other jobs that I would never otherwise have been considered for.

One of those jobs was the PA announcer for the Utah Starzz. I remember the phone call I got from the front office of the Starzz. I was practicing law at the time, and the kind man on the other end of the phone was flattering (something I didn't hear a lot of during my time at the law firm). He said, "Amanda, Larry Miller is buying a WNBA franchise, and he wants you to be the PA announcer."

"Great!" I said with excitement. "What's that?"

"Well, it's the 'Bring 'em on out! How 'bout this Jazz!' guy, only female."

"Great," I answered again, completely unsure of what I was getting myself into. "But I don't know anything about basketball."

"It's not rocket science, Amanda. It's a game. You'll have fun.

That's just what we want you to do—come out and have a good time."

"I'll be there!" (This was during my say yes and ask questions later phase.)

I remember showing up to the Delta Center on my first night. I got to park in the back with all the big black SUVs. That was plenty exciting enough. And then I got to walk around on the lower level of the arena, thinking, *Magic Johnson walked here!* I found my way to center court and met the very talented guy who announces the Jazz games, Dan Roberts. He knew everybody—the officials, the ushers in green jackets, the cheerleaders, the guys with walkie-talkies.

"You ready for this?" he asked. He seemed like a good-natured guy.

"Hope so." I was starting to get nervous now.

"Ah, c'mon. It's easy. Here's the sheet. This is your bible. Just follow along with me. You see these columns here? This is the player's name. Here's her number. Here's her position. Here's her height. Here's her weight."

I said, "That's rude."

He continued, "And here's her university or country of origin. Now—you just go like this and let your voice get slowly bigger until you get to the name—and then you give it your really big voice. Okay?"

"You bet."

"All right—just as an example—you'd say, 'Starting at center. Wearing number 12. At 7'2". From Russia.' Now your biggest voice, 'Margoooooooo Dyyyyyyydekkkkkkkk!!'"

"Oh. I get it." I was catching on now. "We're like Charlie Brown's teacher. People have no idea what we're saying, but if we say it in that voice—they will clap. Blah! Blah! Blah! Blah! Blah! Blah! Blah! Blah!" (I ended in a very big voice.)

Silence.

Oops.

I'm thinking Dan did not appreciate that analogy.

Just as I was wondering what a clueless lawyer like me was doing in the middle of this kind of excitement, the dancers did one final routine and skipped off the floor, the flying blimp that had been dropping prizes went back to its corner, and it was time for the tip-off. The music was loud, so loud, and the fans were on their feet. And then we were off.

UUUUGGGHHHHH!! Who's got the ball? Wait. That was a whistle. Who blew the whistle? The officials are the shortest people on the court. By the time I've got the right guy, he's walking at me making signals that remind me of someone directing traffic on an aircraft carrier. *Can't he just tell me who the foul is on? I'm two feet away from him.*

I screwed up something terrible that first night, and regularly throughout the first season. There was so much to learn. Hand signals and rules. Buzzers and whistles. Offensive and defensive fouls and being in the penalty. That first night I think I got one foul wrong three times in a row. On the third try I said in my best booming voice, "I'm sorry. The foul is on number 32." A guy clear in the top of the arena yelled down in an even better booming voice, "That's—Okay—Amanda!" Right. It's about having fun.

A few years later, the team packed up and moved to San Antonio. So technically, I didn't get fired. A bunch of us lost our jobs when the team left, and many fans lost their spirit. Maybe I should have been fired. But the point is—see all of the crucial information you acquire even when a job doesn't work out? This is good stuff. You usually have to pay for stuff this good. And before I glamorize failure any more than I already have, let me say there is crucial information in *not* being fired as well. If you're not fired today, if you continue to get good reviews, if they keep paying you to do the work or handle the account, then you're getting a big message—your best is good enough.

I've known many people who worry nearly every day that they're going to get fired. The majority of these people have not been fired, at least not so far, but they've worried constantly about it anyway. I tell them what I'll tell you. If you haven't been fired today, your best is good enough. Companies are in business to make money. All organizations want to be successful, and unless you're married to the boss's daughter, they will fire you if you're not helping them achieve their goals. So—just to make sure you've got it—how do you know you're good enough to be the sales manager? Because you are. How do you know you're the best person for the job? Because you've got the job. When they find somebody better, you'll get fired, and he'll get your job. That's the way it works. I've been the one fired and the one doing the firing. Trust me on this one.

When an enormously talented person applies for a job at your company, and there is no immediate opening, your manager looks at the weakest link in her chain and makes a judgment call. Is it better to keep that weak link and hope he improves, or is it better to dump him and train this new person? That's the question. If it's better and more cost-effective to train the new person, and you're the weak link, your boss will fire you and hire the new guy. So—if you didn't get fired today—you're the best person for the job. Don't rest on your laurels about this, but stop worrying about whether you're right for the job. Remember the key—appreciation. Start appreciating your job instead of worrying about it.

And this applies to moms and husbands and wives as well. How many spouses do you know who worry they're not good enough for their husband or wife? I've heard the insecurity in my friends, and in myself: "He's so handsome. He could be with anyone. I wonder why he stays with me." Or "She's so amazing. Everywhere we go, people just love her. I can't imagine what she's doing with me." Or moms who are convinced that they must be the worst mother on earth or at least on the block. Hey—how do you know you're the perfect wife for your husband? Because you *are* the wife. Stop working on not being the wife by doubting yourself—and him—so much. Just appreciate him and you're good to go.

It's been my experience that women struggle with this kind of insecurity a little more than men do. Women I've known are just never satisfied with themselves or their work. Their cooking isn't good enough. Their kids and their cars, their husband's clothes and their fingernails aren't good enough. Their figures aren't perfect enough. Women think breasts come in two sizes—too big and too small. They think you have to dust with a Q-tip in order to have your house looking nice enough. How many of you women cannot rest until the kitchen is clean? I mean, you may have a fever of 103 degrees, and you'll get out of bed to wash dishes because you just cannot rest until those counters are cleared. I don't say this with criticism. I am the same way. What is that?

It's not thinking our best is good enough. Wait. Check that. It's not *knowing* our best is good enough. This is a lesson I am learning and relearning every day. I have two particularly good teachers who help me with this. My son Cameron and my daughter Ashley. Cameron is not intimidated to try new things, to express new ideas, to shoot video of himself hosting his own Food Network show. He doesn't second-guess how people will respond to what he says.

He just says what he thinks and trusts that it's good enough. Like the other day he tried out his new "Fruit Theory" on me. Ashley asked me, "Have you heard Cameron's fruit theory?"

"Fruit theory?" I replied.

"Well, yeah," Cameron answered. "I've figured out why I don't like big fruit, like oranges and apples and bananas, but I do like little fruit, like grapes and raspberries and strawberries."

"Okay," I said, taking the bait. "And why is that?"

"Because big fruit requires too much commitment."

I pictured myself consoling his ex-girlfriends in years to come.

Ashley has a wonderful ability to make me feel good about myself. In fact, I wish I could give to her what she gives to me in this regard. She is so beautiful, so talented and remarkable in so many ways, but she doesn't see it. When she looks at herself, she sees average—sometimes below average. She was told when she was a child that she had a learning disability, and now sometimes that's all she sees. I wish I could go back in time and never let her see that doctor. I can only wonder how her life would have been different without that debilitating diagnosis.

Maybe I worry too much. She is sixteen, and I know most sixteen-year-olds doubt themselves every day, every minute. Just this afternoon we were having lunch before she had to go to work. (Yes. She has her first job at PetSmart. Isn't that wonderful?) I was complaining about not being able to get started in my writing today.

"How many chapters do you have done?" she asked.

"Ten," I answered.

"How many are you doing total?" she kept going.

"Thirteen."

"So, you're almost done," she encouraged.

"I guess. But as I'm writing, I keep thinking—'Who would ever want to read this? It's just my thoughts and my experiences about work and life. Who cares?'"

"Well," she said as if it were so obvious, "people would buy Oprah's book, and they'll buy yours for the same reason."

In my wildest dreams. But wasn't that great?

I want to share one more thought with you on doing your best, and accepting that your best is good enough. This one is about a judge who used to sit on the federal bench in Utah. His name was Judge Ritter. I did not have the pleasure of appearing before him myself when I was a lawyer, but the stories about him were so plentiful during that time, and one of them comes to mind right now.

First I should tell you that Judge Ritter was crazy. (Was that too strong?) I mean, if there were construction workers outside using a jackhammer on Main Street in front of the courthouse, and the jackhammers were interrupting his train of thought, he'd send the bailiff out to get the jackhammer guys and bring them into the courtroom, where he'd make them sit all day! Or then there's the story of the lawyer Judge Ritter didn't like who appeared before him regularly. At the end of one case, the judge asked the lawyer's client in open court, "Sir. Do you have a quarter?"

The client appeared confused. The judge wanted to borrow a quarter? He felt around in his pockets, found one, and held it out toward the bench.

"Give that to your attorney," Judge Ritter pronounced. "Counsel, You've been paid."

Haaaa!!!!!

But that's not the story I wanted to tell you. The story I wanted to tell you was about an elderly man who was appearing before Judge Ritter for sentencing after being convicted on two federal felonies. Many of you may know that in the federal system, there is very little discretion permitted a judge (at least there was very little when I was practicing). There's a graph with your criminal history (if you have one) on one side, and the severity of the crime (judged by dollars or the amount of drugs involved) on the other side. Wherever those two lines meet is how long you go away for. In this case, there was a great deal of money involved.

The judge said, "I hereby sentence you to twenty years in the federal penitentiary, as I am required to do by law. Does the defendant have anything to say to the court?"

The older man stood up slowly, "Well, yes, I do, Your Honor . . . Are you nuts? I'm 76 years old. I am never gonna serve twenty years in the federal penitentiary!"

Judge Ritter leaned out over the bench and said, "Do the best you can!"

So, do the best you can, and remember—your best is good enough.

CHAPTER TWELVE

Just Breathe

"It's not the hours you put in your work that count, it's the work you put in the hours."
—Sam Ewing

I've never quite understood the definition of overachiever. If an overachiever is someone who performs more or better than expected, I think *expected by whom,* or *more or better than what?* That term has been used to describe me before with what felt like disapproval. When that's happened, I've always wanted to say, "Well, how much achievement would be all right with you?" I suppose I'm guilty as charged, at least by someone's definition. Giving birth to two children while in my 40s probably qualifies me on some list. But I am not an overachiever by my own definition, which is the only definition I'm interested in (except for maybe my husband's).

I am not an overachiever for one key reason. I rest. I stop, I rest, and I just breathe. I say no, and I rest. I love this part, although I should admit to you that it used to make me so uncomfortable I would itch. Let's see if any of this rings a bell with you.

When I was a lawyer, I was so uptight I could not enjoy time off. Not an evening, not a weekend, and definitely not a week's vacation. I remember taking photocopied cases with me to college football games so I could read with a highlighter pen during time-outs. (I took an enormous amount of heckling for this, by the way.) I would want to enjoy an evening out with my husband, but every movie we saw, every conversation we had, wound up coming back to a case, which probably meant I was starting an argument. One Sunday in particular stands out in my mind because it was snowing, hard, and I pushed through to get to the office. I got there and made it soaking wet to the elevator, which I found out of order. Not one of the four elevators that went to my floor would operate. I pushed the button again and again with varying degrees of firmness to try to get it to work. I called security, who called the repairman, but it wasn't going to get fixed anytime soon. I felt as though I was going to cry. I felt desperate. What would I do if I couldn't work that Sunday?

I should have awakened right then. That ridiculous moment should have been enough to kick me off the track of excess and obsessive work I was on. "Hey! Amanda! Wake up. You're missing your life." But nooooooo. It took years after that. Years and so much pain, for myself and my family.

I got sick on vacations, irritated with sporting events that went into overtime, frustrated with friends who just wanted to talk. I ate at my desk, sometimes three meals a day, and probably too many snacks in between because I gained weight. And mind you—none of this overachieving made me a better lawyer. I wasn't good to begin with and probably got worse as the months turned into years. So why was I doing it? Why did I give up all of my precious life for work I did not find joy in or excel at? Why couldn't I rest?

It's the same reason why for years in my radio career, I found myself unable to say no to any request. Want me to lose weight in public for Jenny Craig? Sure. Want me to wear your clothes, drive your car, eat at your restaurant, sleep on your bed, remodel my bathroom, read your book, eat your eggs or cheese or sausage, color my hair, stop coloring my hair? Of course. Whatever you like. Want me to emcee your events at night (for free), even though I get up at 2:45 in the morning? Absolutely. That's my duty to the station and to you.

I simply could not say no. And I mean no disrespect to any of the clients or individuals who made these requests of me. It was a perfectly acceptable and expected thing for them to ask. They should do that. That's their job. My job is to know how to balance my own life. That's not anybody's job but mine. When I look back at those years, I feel so grateful for all of the opportunities I was given. And I feel most grateful of all for the balance I finally learned.

It took having children for me to ultimately get it. All of the exhaustion and dissatisfaction and letting people I loved down didn't do it for me, until I became a stepmom. Then suddenly I learned balance. The children were my personal gurus. Like the Buddhists say, "When the student is ready, the teacher will appear." Perhaps I was ready at long last, because there they were, and they knew exactly what to say or do to show me to myself.

Early on in my relationship with their father, I would work nearly every Saturday. Weekends were our only time together as a family back then. Aaron asked me one day, "Are you going to work every time the kids are here?"

"No. Of course not," I answered, starting to feel defensive.

"Well, you have been," he said with kindness, but clearly looking for something. "And the kids are starting to wonder if you don't want to be with them."

Ouch. They really thought that? I didn't feel that way. I loved being with them, even when we did nothing and just made fun of infomercials on TV. I loved our Saturday morning feasts with funny looking tomatoes from the farmer's market. I loved listening to them play SimCity or RollerCoaster Tycoon on the computer. But I wasn't showing them. To them, it felt as though I was avoiding them by working every Friday night and Saturday morning.

"Then I'll stop," I said. And I did. Just like that. It was such a strong realization that I stopped cold turkey. I've heard of people stopping smoking just like that. Not many, but some. They'll be driving down the road and suddenly the cigarette they light up tastes dirty and dry, and they're done. Or their daughter comes to them and says, "Please quit smoking, Mom and Dad. I want you to stay alive." That's it. They're done. And so was I.

In order to have joy in your work, you must value rest. It's sort of the same thing as how you cannot see the light without the darkness. You can't value and excel at productivity without the absence of it. And I know this is a hard thing for many moms and dads to hear. You go, go, go. You take your kids to every game, every lesson, every recital. You help with all the homework, bake brownies, coach the Little League team, make the Halloween costumes. You do it all, every day, day after day—and you'd never complain. This is your joy, not just your job. You were born to play this role and you love every minute of it. I hear you.

And you still must rest. You most of all. You who are rearing the next generation, showing them how to live, loving them into adulthood and all of its challenges—you must rest. Tonight you put the kids down early, take a bath, put your pajamas on and rest. This weekend you ask your neighbor to watch your kids on Saturday, and you go to the library and read until you lose track of time. You take a deep breath every time you notice your brain trying to make a list. You take a deep breath every time you remember a bill that needs paid or a phone call that needs to be made. Your plants can wait, and so can your sales reports. Rest.

And don't think for one minute during this rest that you're ignoring your kids or you should be with them—even if the little one cried when you walked him to the neighbor's. You are loving them when you love yourself. You've heard this before but you never believed it. Believe it from a fellow mom who knows the only way I keep loving my kids well every day is to take time to rest. I would snap without it. I would daydream and forget their schedules without it. I would not see their smiles without it. I rest.

My brother explained it to me this way once, and it really helped. "You have to put your own oxygen mask on first, Amanda, before you can assist your children." I remember the day he said that. I just stopped. It felt as though I had been running as long as Forrest Gump did in that unforgettable movie—from coast to coast and back again. And then there was silence and stillness. Put my oxygen mask on first. I was pushing so hard I had been running out of breath and didn't realize it. If I kept going at that pace, I wouldn't be able to help the children. I wouldn't be able to shop for them, feed them, listen to them, help them with anything. I needed oxygen. I needed rest.

And for you overachievers out there, I know you believe that you can never let down. You have to go and go and push and push. You have to work weekends to get noticed. You're on a career ladder and you've got momentum, baby! I hear that, and I can feel your passion. Keep it going, but get out your calendar right now and put down at least five hours of rest somewhere in the next month. Schedule it in. Pick a Saturday or Sunday or holiday and block out the whole day. Don't let anything get in the way of that day. Schedule babysitters or whatever you need to do to have that time entirely to yourself. Your kids will understand. Your spouse will understand. Your supervisor will understand. She's been wondering when you were going to burn out. It will do her faith in you good to see the wisdom and maturity in your behavior. And this advice from a fellow professional who wants to be known as the hardest-working woman (person) in the office. Well, the only way I do that, achieve that, deliver that for my ownership is to rest. My managers want me to rest. They know they have a clutch player in me, but I'm not worth anything to them, let alone what they pay me, if I'm not on my "A" game. I owe it to them to get my sleep and heal my spirit. I rest.

And rest is different for each of us. I'm not telling you that you have to nap (although doesn't that sound wonderful?). Rest is whatever slows your heartbeat, whatever takes you out of your to-do lists, whatever makes you stop thinking and analyzing and "working it." Walk in the park. Paint. Sleep. Bathe. Go to the spa. Drive and listen to your favorite music that nobody else in the family likes. Swing on a porch. Rest. If you're new to this, prepare to feel awkward, perhaps even guilty. Prepare to itch and fidget and check the clock and wonder if you're dropping the ball while you're doing it. If you have any of these sensations, you're on the right track. I'd tell you to take a class or listen to a tape on meditation (which is probably a great idea), but then I'd be a hypocrite because it's never worked for me. I've tried, but I can't get that still.

The one thing I did learn from meditation was the breathing. The key to rest is in the slowing of the breath. Childbirth brought this point home to me. When I would be in pain toward the end of my pregnancies, I would breathe. Just breathe. The contraction will pass. The discomfort will pass. The baby will stop standing on my bladder, and it will pass. Just breathe. Then I remembered what I had learned about meditation—it's the same thing. We slow, we breathe, we rest our minds and bodies. And in the rest there is power.

Yes, power. I know some of you stockbroker, deal-making, red-eye-flying productivity junkies are thinking this chapter on rest is for sissies. *Au contraire!* It feels counterintuitive, I know. It feels all wrong, lazy even, wasteful. I know. Do it anyway. Do it *because* it feels uncomfortable. You know the adage about how we must walk toward that which we fear. You fear downtime?—walk toward it. You fear what you will feel (insecure, probably) if you stop working 24/7; why not find out? You fear getting to know your wife and kids again if you actually go home without a briefcase full of work, run toward it. You'll find they've been waiting for you.

I think I'm writing this chapter because I need to hear it more than you do. I've learned this lesson before, but as with so many other important principles, I seem to need to learn it over and over again. I've worked, burned out, quit. I've overachieved, dazzled people, then dropped the ball in physical collapse. I'm probably pushing a little too hard right now, trying to get this book done before the baby comes, but I have those two deadlines looming so large that I can't slow down just yet. At least that's what I think until my body throws me for a loop and reminds me that I'm not in charge of anything. Nothing like being hooked up to tubes in the hospital, stranded with bad daytime television and no Doritos to really remind you—you are not in control.

Isn't that one of the grand lessons you learn from pregnancy or any kind of illness or physical challenge? It is such an illusion to think we are in control. We are not. You could fall over today from a malady you didn't know you had until that moment. Someone could do something that completely rocks your world, like the insurance commercials where the two girls are driving along and suddenly get hit by a car. I remember feeling jolted the first time I saw that ad. It jolted me, and it reminded me, we're not in control.

All the more reason to rest. Just breathe. Remember? Bless and release.

CHAPTER THIRTEEN

Surprise! Surprise!

"Success usually comes to those who are too busy to be looking for it."
—HENRY DAVID THOREAU

So here's a hypothetical—you're driving to work tomorrow morning, and you die. You weren't planning to die, of course, but you do. You're in a massive car accident, and it's the end of your life. You hear about these accidents on the news every morning, accidents that divert traffic and slow the commute. Well, this time it's you. And the thought you have before you leave this world is, *Not today!*

Not today. You have so much going on. You're too busy to die today. You were just starting to connect with your teenage son. You hadn't apologized to your wife for the weeks of not listening to her. You were just getting started in your career. In fact, you had a big meeting scheduled for later that morning. You might have closed the biggest account of your career, maybe a big enough account to get you noticed. Who will get the account now?

The things we might think if the end of this life comes on unexpectedly. We might feel such longing, longing to live. And yet when we are alive with what seems like twenty or thirty or forty years stretched before us, we don't live. Why don't we allow ourselves to truly live? Why do we put off life with procrastination and boredom and blame, and then come crashing into the final moments, having allowed ourselves to live so little? Why do we look at people who dance in the rain and laugh out loud and play on the floor with their children as if they were a little off, when these are the things we will crave when it's over?

David—why weren't you David?

I've heard the admonishment "Safety First" all of my life, and when it comes to driving I know that it's true. But not when it comes to living. When you are following your soul's path, safety is the least safe path. Safety keeps you dry and dead. Safety keeps you reading about other people living, going to movies about other people living, and not living yourself. Safety keeps you crying at television instead of at the joy of your own life.

I've never understood why it's so scary to do the thing your soul longs to do, but I know that for many of us it is. Maybe it's like being called on in class to read our poem when we're in the fifth grade. We dread it. We wrote the poem, and Mom loved it, but we're afraid the other kids will laugh. We're afraid they'll see inside us and won't like what they discover. We don't want to show ourselves. But isn't that why we're here? We're here to write poetry, read poetry, risk being humiliated, drop the pass, love the wrong people, mess up our tidy lives. We're here to live with vigor every day and always want more, but not squander one precious moment in fear and waiting and safety.

It reminds me of what my husband's dentist said once. Aaron went in for a root canal, and after having the nerves removed he felt such relief. He asked the dentist, "Why do we have nerves in our teeth in the first place, when we're perfectly fine, even better off, without them?"

"Design flaw," the dentist replied.

I've always wondered about that. Why do we need to feel pain in our teeth? It doesn't keep us from eating. It doesn't protect the teeth the way pain from touching the stove protects the fingers. We only wind up having root canals anyway, and then we go right on eating whatever we want (and brushing and flossing, of course). So with all due respect to our Creator, why do we have nerves in our teeth?

And why are we so afraid of doing what our soul longs to do? Shouldn't we be driven toward our soul's path instead of away from it? I know, some people are pulled toward the light inside them, but many of us struggle with getting stuck in everyday life and only dream in the wee hours about who we really are. Why isn't there something in us that pushes us toward life? Why don't we find it unbearable to sit and stew and miss out on everything we're here to do? Why isn't our life's work irresistible? Is it a design flaw?

I'm sure there are greater truths I just don't understand at work here, that overcoming inertia to move toward our own reason for being is part of the plan—I just wish this for every human being and don't know why it can't be easier.

Wait. Maybe it *is* easier. Maybe it's just as easy as jumping in and lowering our expectations. It wouldn't be so hard to try out for the football team if you didn't feel the pressure to be Joe Montana. Nothing wrong with wanting to be Joe or Steve Young or Emmitt Smith, but let go of the expectation. Just expect to thrill yourself. That's all. Don't expect crowds chanting your name or million-dollar contracts. Those may come, but just expect to thrill yourself. Expect to find out if this is part of what your soul longs to do.

I remember my first day on the air at a very small radio station owned by a lovely man (as opposed to a Fortune 500 company). My heart was beating so fast. I was breathless. I wondered if my listeners, all seven of them, could hear my knees knocking together under the desk. I read a weather forecast. How badly can you screw up a weather forecast? "Partly cloudy. Highs in the 50s." That's it. I made it out of the booth alive, immediately called my boyfriend to see if he had heard me, and asked him if I sounded okay, saying, "Partly cloudy. Highs in the 50s." He said I was brilliant. Smart guy.

I was blessed at that time in my life, as I probably still am today, with just enough audacity to help me live. I was audacious enough to convince the owner of that small station to give me the morning show after I had only been there a short time. "Breakfast with Amanda," it was called, and it lasted for exactly two weeks. I was so green. I didn't know what you could or couldn't do, should or shouldn't do, so I did everything I wanted to do and acted like I owned the place. It was a thrill. If I had expectations of being the next Don Imus, I don't remember them. All I remember of that time was being thrilled.

And then I got bumped for a real radio announcer with real experience, a dear man named Joe Redburn, who wound up being a good friend and teaching me a lot. I learned how to interview celebrities and authors, politicians and people who wanted to be politicians, regular callers who phoned into the show with something interesting to say. And I learned about myself—how I was different from Joe and other announcers, how I had my own voice.

I got curious, something I encourage you to do about whatever it is that interests you, most importantly yourself. Get curious about why you are the way you are. Rather than judge and put down and pigeonhole, get curious. Rather than apologize for liking the music you like, get curious as to why you do. Rather than trying to like different food or different work or different people, get curious about why you feel the way you do. I got curious about why I felt happy at work, and I tried to figure out how that affected my work, how people responded to me when I felt great. I got curious about the people I interviewed, what made them tick, what they loved, what they dreaded, and why they'd take the time to talk to me.

Curiosity didn't kill the cat. Curiosity woke up the cat—to the fact that she's not a dog! Why do I like mice and furry things and string dancing across the floor? Because I'm a cat. Why do I purr and look so fabulous all the time and hate to get dirty? Because I'm a cat! Why do I love to read books and magazines and blogs and old journal entries? Because I'm Amanda. That's who I am. Now what?

Imagine if young people, our teenagers and their friends, could get curious about who they are in a positive way. Instead of experimenting with drugs or tattoos or breaking their curfews, what if they got curious about why they love guitar players or surfing the Web or using graphics programs? What if they got curious about why they keep a friend who puts them down all the time or why they don't have a lot of friends or why they don't like math? What if we helped them wonder, encouraged them to try new things, to get curious? And remember—we only teach our kids through example—so if they see us being curious, maybe they will be too.

I think curiosity ought to be a requirement for most jobs. I know it helps me be a better wife and mother. Wondering why my husband seems distant is so much better than wishing he would change. It lets me figure out that he's not distant at all. He's just tired or needs to just not be pushed for a while until his spirit revives. Wondering why my kids are bored or frustrated is so much better than assuming they're mad at me or just being bad kids.

When I'm curious I find out that something happened at school that upset them, or that their best friend isn't returning their calls, or that they just feel icky and want me to back off.

One of my favorite jobs of the eighteen I've had is being a teacher. I was so gratified to see the curiosity of my college students. I taught Introduction to Mass Media, a class primarily for freshman and sophomores, and Mass Communication Law, a class most students waited until their senior year to take. Teaching these classes was a thrill for me, but I loved Mass Comm Law the most. It was smaller—only forty to fifty students—and there was time in the two-hour class period to address questions. Their questions were so clever and pointed. I often would not know the answer— but I knew where to look. Together we learned how to research answers to our questions, legal and otherwise. We learned how to look at cases, make arguments, address the issues that captured their attention. This was an area of the law that had always captivated me (freedom of speech, libel law, advertising law), and I thoroughly enjoyed relearning it through their eyes.

These students reminded me of the power of curiosity. Curiosity cements learning. When they were curious about a subject, whether because they thought it really applied to what they might do someday as reporters or whether because they were just interested in the subject, they learned. I learned. What we discovered together was more interesting and more applicable to our lives. Their papers were better, their test scores went up, and many of my former students still e-mail me today. We were blessed to have each other for that brief moment in time and to be curious about life and law together.

If you don't love your work right now, get curious. If you love your work but want to figure out how to make more money, get curious. If you want to stay in your present job but you just want to enjoy it more, get curious. That is one of the many extraordinary things about my current job as a morning radio announcer. This job has built-in curiosity. We are a news station, and I interview three or four people every morning about breaking stories. I've got to get curious about the story in order to do my job. I've got to ask them something. I can't just leave Senator Orrin Hatch hanging there on the line without a question, and I can't ask him who he likes in the game this weekend (although I think I have asked that one before). I've got to read several newspapers every morning, peruse several Web sites, read my e-mail, do some research, talk to the reporters and producer and figure out what's going on—and I've got to do it all before five A.M. Being curious is a job requirement for me—and such a blessing.

It was years ago when I first realized why my radio job is so good for my spirit. I recognized that it forces me to be in the moment. If I begin daydreaming about the future or worrying about the past, I lose sight of what's happening. I hit the wrong button or read the wrong thing. *Where am I? Am I supposed to read this story or is it my partner's turn? Is it time for sports or traffic? Should I talk or shut up?* If I let my mind wander, it all turns into a blur. So I have to stay in the moment—and that keeps me where I need to be—spiritually as well as professionally.

I hope this is a skill I've developed for life. I hope whenever the day comes for me to move on from this job and explore some other work, that I have the habit of being present in every moment of my life. I will owe a debt of gratitude to this profession for having taught me such a valuable lesson, such an important skill.

If curiosity doesn't come naturally in your job, you've got to find it. It's there somewhere—just hidden. If you've been teaching the same subject for twenty years to students who seem like the same people year after year, maybe you're not looking deep enough. How does the changing world change your subject, the examples you use in class and on tests, the way you interact with parents? Just for the heck of it, throw all your old lesson plans away and start from the beginning. (Okay—that might be insane.) Turn yourself on about the subject matter and see how it comes out differently.

Imagine what it's like to be meeting you for the first time, coming into your store for the first time, having a legal problem for the first time. Seek the beginner's spirit, but bring to bear the wealth of experience you have accumulated. Have a different conversation with your assistant or your boss. Ask what it's like to work with you and then really listen to the answer. Look at your job as if you were designing it and see where you could improve it. Are you really needed? Are you needed in an area where you're not currently serving, but maybe should be? Are you doing more than you should and sacrificing accuracy? Are you seeing the people around you, really seeing them, and helping them find joy in their work?

One of the glorious things about being forty before bearing children for the first time is that I am brought to my knees by how much I don't know. (I'm also brought to my knees by the fact that I'm too old to keep up with them!) By the time you hit forty, as many of you know, you start to think you know a thing or two. You don't worry so much about looking stupid. If you have a question, you just ask it. Who cares what the waiter or shop clerk or librarian thinks? You appreciate the knowledge you're accumulating. It helps you see the world in a more complete way. Once you've traveled, you appreciate differences in people and cultures more. Once you've stood in Times Square or driven over the Coronado Bridge, you're never quite the same.

But, oh—nothing opens your mind and your heart like having children. Most of you were probably smarter than me and figured this out decades ago, but that was an experience I didn't have until later than most people. I had so much to learn about everything— and still do. How sweetly humbling it is to watch my son cry and have no idea what to do to help him. It rocks my world when he pushes away my attempts to hug him and reaches for his father instead. It brings grateful tears to my eyes every time he puts his little arms around my neck and gives me one of his wet, open-mouth kisses. (He hasn't figured out yet that you're supposed to keep your lips together when you kiss.)

Being a mother is my eighteenth and most thrilling job of all. I find myself wishing every once in a while that I had started when I was younger so I could have had a whole bunch of kids. They delight me. Putting their little legs inside their jammies feels so good. Seeing all of their baby teeth so small and white when they laugh gives me a kick. Watching them interact with each other, even when they're grumpy, fills me with pride. (Those are my grumpy kids. Aren't they great?) There could not be a more fulfilling job than this. I will feel grateful for every moment I get to spend loving my children, whether I am blessed with a long life with them or only a precious few moments. I think it wasn't until my son Ethan was born that I realized I could die today and be happy. I have had the richest life. Yes, I want more—as much as I can get. But if I find myself in that accident today on the way home from work, I will thank God that I got to love my husband and my children at all.

The job of mother comes with joy built in. We moms don't need to search for the joy quite so hard. We need only look into our children's eyes when they're crying and touch them on the cheek, tell them everything is going to be all right. The joy comes flooding in. We need only notice how our son sometimes looks so much like his father that loving our little one feels like loving our husband when he was a little boy. In fact, we have so much joy built into our sacred jobs, we need to spread it around and help the other people in our lives see it and feel it in their own lives. We have enough to share.

If it is joy you seek in your work and your lives, if that is what you truly want, that is precisely what you will have. You will begin today, this moment. There is no need to wait for any change of circumstance. Begin where you are. Then make decisions from that place. Change your job. Don't change your job. Either way, you have already decided to make joy your co-worker and companion in all that you do.

Then, when people ask why you're so happy all the time, you'll know what to tell them. "I don't know any other way." Your co-workers will see it in you. It may irritate them, but it will bless them anyway. More importantly, your spouse and your children will see it in you. Instead of wondering if they're the reason you're so unhappy all the time, they'll wonder if they're the reason you're so happy all the time. What a wonderful thing for the ones you love to wonder! Nothing you ever do will teach them better how to lead happy lives than watching you lead one.

So wash dishes. Clean bathrooms. Go to work. Get fired. Get promoted. Do it all. As Bob Dylan said, "Get up in the morning and go to bed at night and in between do what you want to do."

And let the joy pour in.

INDEX